MURDER *of the* JUJUBE CANDY HEIRESS

MURDER *of the* JUJUBE CANDY HEIRESS

A Coronado Cold Case

TAYLOR BALDWIN KILAND

THE
History
PRESS

Published by The History Press
Charleston, SC
www.historypress.com

Front cover, inset: Ruth and Charles Quinn as they embark on their honeymoon cruise, New York City, October 30, 1930. *Quinn family*; *inset*: Picture postcard of the famous Hotel del Coronado. *Coronado Historical Association Collection.*

Back cover, inset: Ruth Quinn in her senior year of college, in 1921, at the Trinity College for women in Washington, D.C. *Archives Trinity Washington University*; *top*: Orange Avenue in the 1970s. *Tommy Lark Photograph Collection; Coronado Public Library.*

First published 2025

Manufactured in the United States

ISBN 9781467150583

Library of Congress Control Number: 2024949820

CONTENTS

Contents

ACKNOWLEDGEMENTS

In the summer of 2003, while attending a July 4 barbecue in Coronado, California, I was discussing the island's quirky history of crime with Susan Keith. She is a third-generation Coronado resident, a former city councilwoman and one of the island's matriarchs. Our families have been friends for many years, and the men in our families have served together over multiple generations in the U.S. Navy in several wars.

In between our burgers and potato salad, we were discussing some of the strange characters on our island. I reminded her of a break-in of my Coronado apartment in 1993, when a thief stole only one type of item from my home: my underwear.

Single and living alone at the time, I was unnerved. To my knowledge, the thief was never caught. That led to a discussion of the Coronado Police Department and their track record of solving island crimes.

At that point in the conversation, Susan paused. She leaned in and asked me somewhat conspiratorially, "Have you heard of the unsolved murder of Ruth Quinn?"

I had not.

My family was not living on the island when it occurred in 1975. We *did* spend a lot of time here that year because my grandmother was dying of emphysema, which killed her in September 1975. But I was only eight years old.

In 2003, however, I was intrigued. Why was it never solved? Why was a weapon never found? What was the motive? Who knew what and when? Where did it happen? *And who was Ruth Quinn?*

That summer, I started digging into this cold case. I began my research with microfiche at the Coronado Public Library. By the time I finished writing this book in 2024, I could search all California newspapers on the internet from the comforts of my home office. In 2003, Ancestry was a publishing company collecting genealogy research and family trees on the internet. 23andme.com did not exist. Now, of course, these are massive DNA databases being used to solve cold cases. In 2003, two of the three of the main suspects were alive. Many of the characters in this story were too. Now, all three of the main suspects have died, and many other figures germane to the case have also passed.

Life got in the way (a marriage, a baby, a few other books), and I set this project aside for fifteen years, where, like the case, it gathered dust. During the pandemic, I blew on it and opened Pandora's box once again. The result is based on first-person interviews, primary source materials, personal collections of documents and photos and lots of fifty-year-old memories.

Most instrumental in the research and leads in this story has been Joe Ditler, a longtime island local who was also a suspect in the case—if only for a nanosecond. Joe was an early collaborator and coinvestigator of this case and book. His early research was invaluable.

Also instrumental was a cousin of the Heide family who was so generous with her time and perspective on this complicated family. She is one of the most kind, generous and empathetic individuals I have ever met.

In addition to Susan Keith, another island local and my father's childhood friend Dr. Vince Flynn introduced me to all the characters of this story. He remembers absolutely everything. His leads and insight were immeasurable.

I owe many thanks to myriad locals and friends who lent an ear, gave their perspective and feedback and advice and shared their dirt, including my mom and Papa, Anne Kiland and Captain Ing Kiland, Kelly Andrade, Amy Argetsinger, Betsy Bird, Detective Lisa Brannon, Anna Burrous, Michael Callahan, Sergeant Tim Chantler, Steve Collins, Paul Dodson, Lee Dorsey, Penny Duermeyer, John Elwell, Rear Admiral Jim Flatley, Abigail Fleming, Beth Fleming, Monica Flynn, Pat Flynn, Sefton Graham, Judy Gray, Page and Jeff Harrington, Richard Hartwell, Terry Helm, Candice Hooper, Jamie Howren, Bob Hutton, Cameron Johann, Chief Chuck Kaye, Laurie Krill, Esky Kurtz, Chrissy LeMoyne, Clara Mason, Hal Matthews, Liz McLean, Pike Meade, Maureen Moriarty, Andy Morrison and Barbara Beardsley, Dr. John Morton, Caroline Murray, Bob Paseman, Shannon Player, Valerie Quate, Margo Rhodes and Kimball Worcester, Kim Rius,

Miguel Rodriguez, Patsy Rogers, Louis Shwetzer, DeeDee Slewka, Doug St. Denis, Christine Stokes, Vickie Stone, Emily Talbert, Jay Talbert, Captain Dick Tarbuck, Chris Toogood and Susan Riddle Whiting.

Finally, I must acknowledge my tirelessly tolerant husband and daughter, Mike and KK Hatcher. I love you.

MAIN CAST OF CHARACTERS

This cold case has an odd assortment of suspects and characters:

CORONADO, CALIFORNIA. Across the Bay from San Diego, this island has been home to generations of Navy families whose husbands and fathers (and now wives and mothers) serve at Naval Air Station North Island—the birthplace of naval aviation—and the Naval Amphibious Base Coronado, the home to Navy SEALs. In 1975, the village had few stoplights, one high school, one library, one all-night diner and lots of gossip. It also boasts a historic hotel, the Hotel del Coronado, with its iconic red turrets. The Del is a popular playground for the rich and famous who travel from all over the world to see the Victorian resort perched on the edge of the Pacific Ocean and to experience the island's near-perfect year-round climate. It is seventy degrees and sunny nearly every day.

Coronado is an emerald isle, a paradise for military families, a cocoon in which to wait for the many moms and dads who deploy to war zones for months—or years—on end. The crime rate is low, so no one locks their doors and kids bike everywhere, even late at night. They spend weekends surfing, playing beach volleyball and burning beach bonfires.

RUTH LEYENDECKER QUINN. The seventy-four-year-old retired librarian was an heiress of sorts, the granddaughter of Henry Heide, who was known as the "Dean of American Candy." He was a German Catholic immigrant who made his fortune selling Jujubes and Jujyfruits—movie theater staples for generations of kids. Raised in affluence in Manhattan, Ruth married a naval aviator and had two sons, only one of whom reached adulthood. Like many Navy families, she and her surviving son, Chuck, waited out World War II in Coronado. But she became a widow before the war was over when her husband, Commander Charles Quinn, died of pneumonia in 1945 on his way home from victory in the Battle of the Atlantic.

C<small>HARLES</small> "C<small>HUCK</small>" H<small>ENRY</small> Q<small>UINN</small> J<small>R.</small> Ruth's only surviving son was raised on the beach in Coronado, where he became a top-notch surfer and a lifeguard. He also left a legacy as an expert deep-powder skier in Alta, Utah, where he was a ski instructor for ten winters. Weighed down with mental breakdowns, alcoholism and two children he did not raise or know, he had a difficult time holding down a job and paying his bills.

H<small>ANK</small> L<small>EYENDECKER.</small> Ruth's baby brother followed Ruth to Coronado when he and their mother, Johanna Heide Leyendecker, moved into the Hotel del in 1937. Here, mother and son lived in adjacent guest rooms for the next two decades. Also raised in affluence, Hank was a playboy, living off the family trust inherited from his mother. He never held a paying job. Instead, he spent his days playing tennis and his summers at the oldest dude ranch in the United States, Wyoming's Eatons' Ranch. There, he avoided service in World War II and learned to play the role of a cowboy.

A<small>LAN</small> G<small>RAHAM.</small> Married to Jim Morrison's sister, Alan first came to Coronado with his in-laws, naval aviator Rear Admiral Steven Morrison and his wife, Clara. Here he stayed. Born and raised in gritty Liverpool, England, this Englishman mostly worked as a carpenter when he was not trying to make money off his familial status with the Doors' frontman. He met Ruth in 1971 when she hired him to repair her dining room table.

AN ESSAY ON FREE DIRT

The handwritten sign was perched unobtrusively, short and squat, next to a residential driveway on the corner of a busy intersection. It was mounted on a small stake and shoved crookedly onto a mound of fine, dusty loam.

"Free Dirt," it advertised.

In a town where a twenty-five-foot-wide lot of dirt sells for millions of dollars, this pile on the corner of Fourth Street and Alameda Boulevard was the only free dirt in this expensive town—unless you count the whispered gossip.

A steady stream of cars passed this sign every afternoon leaving Naval Air Station North Island. Up to forty thousand cars buzz along Fourth Street daily, en route to the Coronado Bridge on the Southern California island of Coronado. Residents bemoan the traffic along this road, but they must coexist with the cars. After all, the Navy has been here in Coronado much longer than any of its current residents.

I was sitting at a stoplight on my way to work early one morning in 2003 when I noticed this sign and its irony. It made me chuckle.

My paternal grandparents bought some of this dirt many decades ago. They came to this island, like many other Navy families, when our nation was at war. My grandfather, a 1917 graduate of the U.S. Naval Academy, served in World War I, World War II and the Korean War.

Like many Navy "juniors," my father was dragged around the country during his childhood. His father's career took him to Pearl Harbor;

The author and her father, Captain Ingolf Kiland, at the Hotel del, April 1971. *Author's collection.*

Washington, D.C.; Norfolk, Virginia; and Coronado. He arrived on this island for the first time in 1942, to wait out World War II with my grandmother while my grandfather fought the Japanese in the Pacific. The Navy Cross my grandfather earned during the Battle of Guadalcanal is on display in my living room.

During World War II, the Kilands lived in several homes on the island, including 500 Pomona Avenue, in the neighborhood where this story takes place. Many residents believed Coronado was vulnerable to attack and could be the next Pearl Harbor. My grandmother served as a block captain, patrolling the neighborhood every night to ensure all the residents blackened their windows in a citizens' attempt to foil any potential enemy intent on bombing our island home.

After my grandfather retired from the Navy in 1957, he and my grandmother returned to Coronado and moved into a cottage here. My dad's Navy career also brought us to Coronado for several tours of duty in the 1970s. My mother, my brother and I waited on the island while Papa was deployed to the war zone. *My* Navy service brought me back to Coronado for a tour of duty. The house my grandparents built is now the family homestead, where my parents also retired. My husband and I fully expect to retire here, too. We appreciate the dirt we have inherited. We certainly could not afford it any other way.

This island is decidedly conservative, a bedrock of support for the armed forces who work here. For decades, military service was practically a requirement to be a resident here. The Navy has brought generations of families like mine to Coronado for more than a century. And these neighbors are still recognized around town by their rank. Their idiosyncrasies, sins and even their crimes can be overlooked—because they are war heroes or married to war heroes or related to war heroes. And their stories make for some great dirt. Rich dirt. Free dirt.

A Map of the Murder
CORONADO in 1974-1975

A Map of the Murder: (1) Ruth Quinn's home, (2) The Millers' home, (3) Sacred Heart Catholic Church, (4) Coronado Public Library, (5) Coronado Police Department, (6) Alan Graham's home (in 1975), (7) Laura Christian's home, (8) Coronado Hospital, (9) North Beach, (10) Hotel del Coronado. *Author's collection.*

1

TAPS ON POMONA

Fifty years ago I learned a verse which is very applicable today: "Ah, you are strange, inscrutable and proud, I cannot prove you, though I try and try. But you will keep my love alive and wondering until I die." God keep you in His loving care.
—1971 letter from Ruth Quinn to her son Chuck Quinn

The drip, drip, drip on Ruth Quinn's dining room table from the leak in her bungalow's roof was particularly annoying. And she probably knew she was going to have to get a little pushy about it.

She had already spent money having the table repaired *once*. What's more, the rakish carpenter she had hired to fix it had performed shoddy work, in her opinion. And then he had added insult to injury by invading her home and robbing her.

That was four years ago. Now, she sighed, the dining room table was going to need more repairs. And that, she decided, needed to be remedied.

Despite her reputation as an heiress, Ruth was only a renter. The granddaughter of the "Dean of American Candy" Henry Heide was a good Catholic girl raised on the Upper West side of Manhattan with nannies, maids and chauffeurs and sent on a European tour after college. But her days of opulence were far behind her. Ruth was now living on a fixed income.

Ruth had been renting homes from Cynthia "Cinnie" Heyer and her brothers, Ezra and Dick Parker, for several years. Their extended family owned multiple properties on this block of the Southern California island of Coronado.

The Coronado bungalow Ruth rented from 1968 until she was murdered on March 16, 1975. *Author's collection.*

She had lived in this cozy home at 511 Pomona Avenue since 1968. It was a small white clapboard cottage, built in 1937 on what is called a "flag lot" because of its shape: a small square lot behind a street-front lot, accessible by a long driveway, which makes it look a lot like a flagpole.

The structure, which is largely extant today, has two bedrooms and one bathroom, a rusty screen door and a carport. In front of it in 1975 was an empty lot that was shaded with trees, bushes and another carport shared by her neighbors.

"I love the house and patio, as you know," she wrote to her landlord, Mrs. Heyer, in 1969. "I hope most sincerely that I will never have to leave—except to my last resting place at [Fort] Rosecrans [Cemetery]."

How prescient she was.

She filled that patio she loved so much with dozens of potted plants: juniper, bottlebrush, oleander, plum, geranium, azalea, variegated holly, asparagus fern, ficus, begonias, grape ivy, lilies and an olive tree.

This was her little private oasis where she could soak up the sunshine, read books and listen to the birds—the seagulls squawking overhead and the hummingbirds, blackbirds, finches and sparrows that made appearances in her garden. "My chief pleasure these days I find in the birds singing so joyously all around the house."

Behind 511 Pomona were the backyards of several more spacious homes that faced Glorietta Boulevard, the wide and grand avenue that lined the perimeter of the island's golf course. All the houses in this neighborhood were tightly packed side by side and back-to-back with postage stamp–sized yards and short fences dividing them all. Residents could hear their neighbors, especially if they were shouting—or firing a weapon.

Today, Cinnie Heyer was in town. She arrived in her brand-new Mercedes and came over midafternoon to visit Ruth and inspect the pesky roof in person.

While she was visiting Ruth and discussing roof repairs, a friend and fellow parishioner arrived with flowers from the Altar Society that Ruth had purchased earlier in the day at church.

Ruth's Sundays usually followed a strict routine: worship, followed by dinner and the Shirley Temple Theater on television.

Sunday, March 16, 1975, started out no differently.

The religious home for island Catholics, Sacred Heart Church was built in 1921 by renowned architect Irving Gill. *Coronado Historical Association Collection.*

On this early spring day, Ruth had attended the morning Mass at Sacred Heart. A creature of habit, she showed up faithfully every Sunday, usually occupying the same pew. She was always formally dressed, with her gray hair on top of her head, clipped into place, with a few stray wisps framing her face. Parishioners knew her from behind.

In fact, all the Catholics on the island knew one another, as there was only one Catholic church on the island: Sacred Heart.

Designed by renowned twentieth-century architect Irving Gill, the Mediterranean-style structure was built in 1921, and it is still the religious home for most Catholic residents in Coronado.

Ruth was devout, and her faith had provided routine and comfort throughout her seventy-four years—a life that had served up a heavy burden of tragedy. But this only deepened her faith.

After Mass, she joined her fellow parishioners for a church breakfast. She lived only a few blocks from the church, so she might have walked there.

In the Lenten season, Ruth routinely went back for a second Mass, which she did this Sunday after a visit to the Coronado Library, where she had served as the acting city librarian, the last position she held before she retired in 1959. Many in the island community remember her, despite her short tenure. They reminisce about her loud scoldings when they were

CORONADO LIBRARY   -   CORONADO, CALIFORNIA

The Coronado Public Library, built in 1909, where Ruth Quinn served as the city librarian from 1958 to 1959. *Coronado Public Library.*

children—to "shush," or to stay away from the banned books held behind the librarian's desk.

Or maybe they just remember her untimely demise.

During her second visit to Sacred Heart at the end of the day, a witness noticed her, lost in prayer, until almost 6:00 p.m.

She was never seen or heard from again.

Around 6:57 p.m., as the sun was setting, a few beachcombers lingered and stared at the ocean, waiting for the elusive green flash—that lightbulb moment some claim to see at the second the sun dips below the horizon.

As it did so, many residents on Pomona Avenue and Glorietta Boulevard noticed the playing of taps at the nearby Naval Amphibious Base. This was a nightly ritual. Around the same time, between 6:45 and 7:00 p.m., a neighbor at 522 Glorietta Boulevard heard gunshots.

Ruth's friend from the library, Katheryn Lloyd, tried calling her four times, between 7:45 p.m. and 9:15 p.m. Katheryn wanted to thank her for attending a retirement party the night before. The phone was always busy.

Ruth was not on the phone. Nor was it off the hook. By the time the bugler finished his last note, Ruth was probably already dead. She lay supine in her bed, clad in a purple dress and leather belt, wearing black high-heel shoes and brown nylon stockings, a gold watch on her wrist and gold earrings in her ears, a plastic hair comb and hair clip in her hair. She was partially covered with a bedspread. Her right arm was resting on her belly. Her left hand and the left side of her face were smeared in blood, and the bedding underneath her body was soaked with blood.

Lying next to her was a pillow, punctured with bullet holes and flecked with powder burns. And in a bowl on her bedside table was a small crucifix with Jesus nailed to the little cross. It was turned over, so the figure of Jesus was not facing her killer.

2

AN ISLAND PARADISE?

Coronado has a dark underbelly.
—*Coronado native and fifth-generation resident Margo Rhodes*

Every town has a rhythm. But you can feel Coronado's only if you are up early, exploring.

The garden sprinklers are the first to stir, before the sun rises. They start with a few drips, followed by a gentle mist that quickly becomes a loud spray. Their chorus echoes throughout the neighborhood with their signature circular "swish, swish, swish." Everyone on this island takes pride in having lush and verdant lawns. Some even pay for the fake kind—spending tens of thousands of dollars to install the crunchy, plastic version that doesn't require a daily soak.

Next up, just as dawn breaks, are the surfers and the stand-up paddleboarders, who brave the sixty-degree waters to catch an early wave in the Pacific or to glide along the shores of the San Diego Bay. Finally, the dog walkers set out on their well-worn paths around the island, coffee cups in hand. On some mornings, beachcombers will be greeted by the sound of a platoon of Navy SEAL candidates jogging by, their boots quietly hitting the soft sand, their breaths in sync with their feet. Or a Navy pilot will roar by, tipping her wings as she flies overhead, low enough to read her plane's tail number.

This island village is just fifteen miles from the Mexican border at the southwestern tip of the United States, but it has a distinct southern

Nimitz-class aircraft carrier USS *Ronald Reagan* (CVN 76) transits the San Diego Bay, as seen from Cabrillo National Monument with NAS North Island in the distance, San Diego, California, July 23, 2024. *U.S. Navy photo by Mass Communication Specialist First Class Keenan Daniels.*

Navy SEAL candidates run with an inflatable boat on their heads during the Hell Week crucible of Basic Underwater Demolition/SEAL (BUD/S) training at Naval Amphibious Base Coronado. *U.S. Navy photo by Mass Communication Specialist Second Class Dylan Lavin.*

sensibility. It is Mayberry on the Pacific: a small town with a lot of character and even more characters. And, like most small-town southerners, everyone in Coronado likes to know about everybody else's dirty laundry. But they do not want anyone airing *theirs*.

With a richly tapestried past in the annals of the military, Hollywood, politics and famous twentieth-century industrialists, the island is also a resort. Coronado boasts a wide and shimmering beach that is consistently rated one of the top ten in the country, as well as the famous Victorian-era Hotel del Coronado—host to presidents, celebrities and film productions.

Only in this village can you witness the landscape juxtaposition of combat aircraft conducting low-level "touch-and-go" landings right over the roofs of $5 million homes and Navy SEALs grunting and groaning through their grueling beach training regimen directly in front of tourists staying at the luxury Hotel del.

Just across the harbor from downtown San Diego, this small island has hosted large personalities. Senator John McCain called it home in the 1940s, along with Cary Grant, Robert Crawford, Johnny Downs, Charlie Chaplin, the Doors front man Jim Morrison, comedian Dick Van Dyke, popular folk and pop band the Kingston Trio and the popcorn magnate Orville Redenbacher. Coronado has also been home to a few murderers, some of whom have never been caught.

When you reach the peak of the sloping Coronado Bridge that connects the city of San Diego to the island, you spy an aviator's view of its small footprint: thirty-two square miles of sand and palm trees. As you descend from the summit of the bridge, you can glimpse off to your left the conic cardinal-red roof of the iconic Hotel del. At night, it emerges from its corner of the island like a glowing pyramid, a beacon for the little suburban village. A mix of Craftsman bungalows, Spanish Revival mansions, Victorian manors and midcentury modern California ramblers line the wide avenues and streets, arranged in an alphabet and numbered grid. The city's "main street" is the meandering Orange Avenue, a wide boulevard named for a grove of orange trees that used to dot its median, along with a streetcar line that disappeared around the same time as the oranges.

The Native American Kumeyaay tribe and a plentiful population of jackrabbits were the first visitors to the island, followed in the 1600s by Spanish explorers who gave Coronado and the other neighboring islands the name Las Yslas Coronadas, or "the crowned islands." In 1885, motivated by Coronado's ideal weather, wealthy midwestern industrialists Elisha Babcock and Hampton Story bought up most of the island for $110,000 and broke ground on a resort hotel, which three years later became the famous Hotel del Coronado.

At the same time, the military was also laying claim to parts of the island. President Teddy Roosevelt sent his Great White Fleet of sixteen battleships to make a port call just off the coast of the Hotel del in 1908. The pioneers of military aviation established a naval air station on the adjacent North Island, building a training base and launch site for many historic firsts. It became known as the "birthplace of naval aviation." Jimmy Doolittle made history with his 1922 flight from Florida to North Island with only one stop. The Navy debuted its first rigid dirigible here, USS *Shenandoah*, and made Coronado the home of its first aircraft carrier, USS *Langley*, in 1924. Charles Lindbergh launched his historic transatlantic quest from North Island in 1927.

Navy SEALs were born and raised on the south side of the island, on what is now the Naval Amphibious Base Coronado. Among the affluent and the famous on the island were lots and lots of these naval and Marine Corps officers, hardy men who made Coronado the home base for their families as they deployed to the Pacific for epic battles in places like Corregidor, Okinawa, Midway, Iwo Jima, Inchon and Hue.

Two or three generations later, many descendants of these early residents dwell in their family homes. The military brought them to the island. The weather motivates them to stay. The heroes of wars past quietly live out their sunset years here. Until 1969, it was still the relatively secluded domain of military families. Tourists arrived every summer for long sojourns at the Del and left when school started. That all changed when the Coronado Bridge was built. The last car ferry ran from San Diego to Coronado on August 3, 1969, the same day that the bridge opened for traffic. Nothing was ever the same. The cars kept coming and have not stopped. The island became more easily accessible, and property values soared.

Today's children and grandchildren of the early military residents who bought their island homes in the twentieth century cling to these valuable assets, keeping up with basic maintenance by renting out garage and alley apartments.

In sharp contrast, Coronado has seen a dramatic invasion of affluent Arizonans (Zonies), Mexicans and Nevadans. They descend on the island every summer with their golf carts and their cash. They have torn down smaller, modest homes—the ones with the twenty-five-foot-wide lots—and built McMansions in their place. The economic landscape has changed. But the old-timers have not. They live on fixed incomes, their money tied

Top: The Coronado ferry crossing the San Diego Bay, circa 1965. It carried both people and cars. *Coronado Historical Association Collection.*

Bottom: Coronado Bridge on opening day, August 3, 1969. *Coronado Historical Association Collection.*

up in the dirt beneath their aging homes. Unlike the gossip in town, this dirt is not free.

They venture out of their homes to walk their dogs, go to the pharmacy or the base commissary, play bridge, get their hair done and perform the "Three Gs" of Coronado: golfing in the morning, gardening in the afternoon and gallivanting at night. For this crowd, gallivanting involves an early cocktail or two on someone's patio or cabana. There, they discuss the latest monstrosity being built in the neighborhood ("A lap pool on the second deck?" "An underground garage with a car turnstile?"). They shake their heads and sip their martinis. Who are these people invading the island? Certainly nothing like them, these long-retired veterans of wars fought long ago.

Coronado is a town that still holds a vintage Fourth of July parade, attracting thousands of fans from all over the county. Armored vehicles and Navy SEALs in full camouflage float down Orange Avenue, buoyed by the crowd's cheers and their waving of the red, white and blue. Coronado relishes its flagrant display of militarism and patriotism and would never apologize for it. And, as long as the old-timers own property here, Coronado will retain some of its Mayberry-era charm.

Until 1973, many of these longtime residents were World War I, World War II and Korean War veterans. Then veterans started coming home from deployments in the Vietnam War. One of the last casualties of that war was a local boy, Marine Corps Captain William Nystul, a 1963 Coronado High School graduate who was killed in May 1975 when the helicopter he was piloting sank into the South China Sea. He had been assisting in the evacuation of South Vietnamese.

Coronado was accustomed to losing its residents in war. They were not desensitized but rather resilient to the inherent hazards of being part of a military community. What Coronado was *not* inured to was murder. And in the year Nystul perished in Vietnam, Ruth Quinn—a seventy-four-year-old World War II widow and retired librarian—was found dead in her bed, fully clothed, with her shoes on, shot execution-style.

3

THE CANDY MAGNATE

Jujubes are one of my favorite frustration candies. Pissed off at someone?
Worry your way through a mouthful of these sticky bastards.
—Jujube candy fan blog

Henry Heide told his family members they should appear in the newspaper only three times: once upon their birth, once upon their marriage and once upon their death. Despite their tremendous wealth during the Gilded Age and the early twentieth century, when many of Heide's peers were making headlines with their fortunes and how they spent them, most of his family abided by this rule. His granddaughter Ruth Quinn was no exception. But the headlines her death generated around the nation were not what her grandfather had in mind:

"Heide Kin, 74, Fatally Shot" —*Central New Jersey Home News*
"Jujube Candy Heiress Slain" —*Morning News* (Wilmington, DE)
"Jujube Heiress Shot to Death in California" —*Kansas City (MO) Times*
"Police Probing Death of Candy Firm Heiress" —*Birmingham (AL) Post-Herald*
"Candy Heir Fatally Shot" —*Danville (VA) Bee*
"Investigate Slaying of Candy Heiress" —*Des Moines (IA) Tribune*
"Candy Heiress Shot to Death" —*Detroit (MI) Free Press*
"Coronado Slaying Remains Puzzle" —*San Diego (CA) Union*

By the time Ruth died, the confectionery empire her grandfather had built was still storied. And his candy creations, especially the Jujube and Jujyfruit candies, had spawned a cult following and generations of candy fans.

It was into a world of vast wealth that Henry Heide's granddaughter Ruth Harriet Leyendecker was born in 1900 in Manhattan. She was the second of four children of a doctor, Philip T. Leyendecker, and Johanna Heide, the firstborn child of Henry Heide.

Ruth and her siblings and cousins were fortunate to get to know their grandfather, the family patriarch. With a full head of white hair, a long white beard, bushy eyebrows and pince-nez spectacles that framed his droopy eyes, he looked the part. He loved to hold court with his grandchildren at his large West Sixty-Ninth Street brownstone, delighting them with ten-dollar gold pieces he bestowed on each of them as treats.

Heide was a German Catholic immigrant of Dutch ancestry. He was the sixth of seven sons of a mayor of the small town of Obermarburg, Germany. Heide apparently felt his prospects would be brighter than his father's if he moved to the United States. As a teenager, he landed in Pittsburgh just after the Civil War, in 1866. For two years, he worked at a retail grocery store there before moving to New York City. In 1869, in a building in what is now SoHo, he

Top: The "Dean of American Candy," Henry Heide. *Quinn family.*

Bottom: Henry Heide with some of his grandchildren, including nine-year-old Ruth (*bottom right*). *Quinn family.*

and another immigrant friend, Herman Blumensaart, began cooking candy from a first-floor apartment they shared. The residence had a plate-glass front window where they displayed and sold small batches.

Wondering if they could expand their market outside their tiny storefront window, they saved their earnings and purchased a wagon and a horse for sixty dollars.

Every day, the two would venture out into their neighborhood, carefully navigating the horse-drawn carriage through the crowded streets of Manhattan. But their horse often bumped into the pillars that supported the elevated trains on First, Second and Third Avenues. Despite their attempts to guide their horse, he seemed very clumsy.

Consulting a veterinarian, they were told the horse was healthy, but, "I thought you two were farming boys?" Well, they *were*, back in Germany. "Didn't you look at the horse's eyes?" the vet asked. Grandpa Heide and his friend glanced at each other and replied, "No. Just his mouth."

Their horse was blind. Yet if they drove him well, he served his purpose. And the candy business grew. Eventually, Blumensaart left the operation to become a Jesuit priest. Heide bought him out, and the Heide Candy Company was born.

He bought a small store on Hudson Street, which he quickly outgrew. His business eventually took over the whole block between Hudson and Vandam Streets, overlooking the Hudson River—a convenient location for shipping products all over the world.

Heide earned early entrepreneurial success with coconut cakes, molasses lumps and cream bonbons. He introduced the first five-cent candy bar in the United States, wrapped in foil. His company also manufactured almond paste, widely used by bakers and chefs to make macaroons and almond confections.

But it was Heide's introduction of Jujyfruits and later, Jujubes (pronounced "Ju-ju-bees"), to the U.S. market in the 1920s that made his brand famous and made him a rich man. Jujyfruits were soft and formed in the shape of vegetables and fruits, like asparagus and bananas. Jujube pastilles came in a variety of flavors like spearmint, lemon, violet, lilac and rose. They were firm and stuck to your teeth.

This candy has been around since the 1700s and was originally made with gum arabic, sugar and a small date-like fruit: the jujube. Also called jujuba, it can be found in many places in the world, primarily in China. Fresh jujube fruit is said to taste like an apple; the dried version is more akin to a date. It is high in sugar content (45 percent). Many thought candies made from the jujube provided medicinal aid, believing that sucking on them like a throat lozenge could reduce coughing fits. Perhaps this is why they were especially popular in movie theaters.

One vintage advertisement promoted the candy's supposed health benefits, providing the Heide's Guide to Happiness:

This 1950s ad for Jujubes and Jujyfruits appeared in a New York magazine. *Author's collection.*

> *1. Sleep eight hours. 2. Sleep on the right side. 3. Have bedroom window open. 4. Place bed against wall. 5. On awakening, take Heide's Assd. Jujubes. They remove the unpleasant taste from the mouth. 6. Take a bath, lukewarm water. 7. Exercise before breakfast. 8. Eat little meat, always well cooked. 9. Eat cereals and starchy foods. 10. At noon take Heide's Mint Jujubes to aid digestion. 11. Avoid intoxicants. 12. Take daily exercise. 13. Drink plenty of water. 14. Limit your ambitions. 15. Restrain your natural character. Don't worry. 16. At night take Heide's Licorice Pastilles. They ensure the respiratory organs and ensure a night's rest.*

Fans today have strong opinions about their preferences for either Jujubes or Jujyfruits. Candy fan blogs wax on about the merits of each:

> *I remember jujubes as one of my all-time favorite candies to eat at the movies. I used to love to stick them on the tip of all my fingers and pretend I had long fingernails. Then I would suck each one off and enjoy the bliss!!!!*

> *Haaaate Jujubes. So flavorless and difficult to eat. The most unrewarding candy ever.*

Never liked Jujyfruits—they actually made me throw up as a kid in the '50s, and I haven't eaten them since. Jujubes, however, are a different story! I can still remember the box: long and white, with the Heide symbol prominently displayed. Yes, they were hard as bricks, but that meant the actual eating process took longer and was more enjoyable.

Jujyfruits are another of my favorite candies—my grandmother always had them in a drawer.

The Heide brand logo—a red and white diamond with the company name emblazoned in the middle—conjured images of childhood, at least for several generations who grew up getting lost in candy stores, five-and-dimes and local movie theaters. The Jujube and Jujyfruit names became synonymous with the entire category of small candies. At one point, seventy-five thousand pounds of Jujyfruits were manufactured weekly.

The company could barely keep up with the demand. "Buying candy is impulse buying," Henry Heide's great-grandson Philip said in 1994. "You don't go to the store with candy on your shopping list. But if you see it before you leave the store, there's a good chance that it will end up in your cart."

By 1925, when Ruth was still living in Manhattan as a young, single, college-educated woman, Henry Heide's company had expanded twelve times. Its 500,000-square-foot factory in Manhattan employed 1,300 people. And Henry Heide became a wealthy man. His extended family, including Ruth and her siblings and her mother, also benefited from his wealth and largesse.

He was known to be a kind and charitable man, one who gave away much of his wealth during and after his lifetime to not only his family but also, notably, Catholic churches and German charities. He raised $250,000 in 1919 for the New York Foundling Hospital and a home for abandoned children established by the Sisters of Charity. That same year, he gave $10,000 to the American Relief Committee for German Children. He was a trustee of the Catholic Charities for the Archdiocese of New York and the Emigrant Industrial Savings Bank and director of the Board of Trade for German American Commerce. He organized the National Confectioners Association. The pope made him a Knight of the Order of Pius IX in recognition of his generosity. And on his seventy-fifth birthday, he received a telegram from Pope Benedict XV for his long-standing support of Catholic charities and "for his constant practice of the Christian virtues." Heide and his wife, Mary Yaeger Heide, had a total of eleven children. When he died in 1931, he gave a significant amount of money to fifty-eight Catholic churches and the rest to his eight surviving children.

After his death, the company was led by a series of Heide descendants until 1995, when it was sold to Hershey's. It was sold again, in 2002, to Farley's and Sather, which merged with Ferrara Pan of Chicago in 2012, creating the Ferrara Candy Company. The Heide name disappeared, but the popular candy he created lives on.

Henry Heide's descendants inherited his fortune. Ruth Quinn's mother, Henry Heide's oldest child, Johanna, never had to work for a living, nor did she need to rely on a husband for her independence. Johanna and her siblings were raised in a formal household where children dressed for dinner. Meals were served punctually in the West Sixty-Ninth Street home by maids. The children were escorted to and from school and Mass by nannies and chauffeurs. They spent their summers at a beach home on the New Jersey shore.

Johanna had met her husband at a dinner party hosted by her parents. She was a gifted musician and had just returned from a trip to Germany to study music, financed by her parents in recognition of her musical talents. Johanna's sister was in love with young Dr. Philip Leyendecker. He was smart and dapper and witty and loved to play practical jokes. But he did not reciprocate the sister's feelings. That evening, Philip instead fell in love with Johanna.

Johanna and Philip married and had three daughters: Marie, born in 1899; Ruth, born in 1900; and Louise, born in 1902. They also had a son, Henry, or Hank, born in 1905. Philip and Johanna's marriage was not a happy one. Being Catholic, they did not entertain divorce. Soon after Hank was born, they agreed to lead separate lives under an agreement reached with the archbishop of New York, Cardinal Patrick Joseph Hayes. Johanna and her children moved out of the family home and into a Manhattan hotel. Eventually, she moved to Coronado, California, where she set up residence at the famous Hotel del. There,

Ruth in her senior year of college, in 1921, at the Trinity College for women in Washington, D.C. *Archives Trinity Washington University.*

she lived for two decades, taking every meal in the hotel dining room and participating in the active party circuit at the hotel.

Ruth and her sisters were educated by the Religious of the Sacred Heart of Jesus, or RSCJ (for the French name Réligieuses du Sacré-Coeur de Jésus), at the Sacred Heart Convent school at Kenwood in Albany, New York. The RSCJ was a religious order with a history of educating wealthy Catholics, especially girls.

This began a lifelong relationship between Ruth and the nuns of the RSCJ, especially one named Mother Genevieve Clarke. After high school, Ruth attended Trinity College in Washington, D.C. And then, like many young women of her class and status, she was sent on a summer sojourn to Europe in 1924. There, on a street in the Netherlands, she met an eligible bachelor and upwardly mobile naval aviator named Charles Quinn.

4

A CHANCE MEETING IN ROTTERDAM

The smiling face that's on this page—the subject of this ditty—is the boy from Forty-second Street and Broadway, New York City. He broke the hearts of all New York and left the girls behind to study hard at Nav, and Juice and all that daily grind....But, fun aside, lest we should make our tale appear deplete, let's wish for him a big career on going in the Fleet. And we can truly say of him and not approach deceit—the friends he's made will last till the Navy's obsolete.
—U.S. Naval Academy Lucky Bag *yearbook entry on Charles Henry Quinn, class of 1926*

I t was a chance encounter. Midshipman Charles Quinn spied two fetching young American girls on the streets of Rotterdam in the summer of 1924. Quinn was a student at the U.S. Naval Academy, traveling to Europe as part of his summer training. His ship had just pulled into port for some "liberty," free time for the crew to blow off steam. World War I was over, and the world was at peace for a while, but the U.S. Navy continued to show off its fleet and exercise diplomacy with port calls around the world. The Netherlands was a close U.S. ally. Shore visits often involved social calls on local government and military officials and parties with local society.

Twenty-four-year-old Ruth Leyendecker and her sister Louise were on their tour of Europe, chaperoned by their aunt. In the grand tradition of European aristocrats, Americans started sending their children overseas to experience the "old country." It was not uncommon in the early twentieth century for young ladies born to a certain amount of wealth to be sent off for an extended tour of the continent. Learning a European language (usually French) and experiencing the art and the food and the culture were essential parts of their education. The overseas trip also served as an introduction to a social scene where they just might meet a husband.

Ruth would never be described as a beautiful woman. She was buxom but not small-waisted, and she boasted soft but not delicate features. But she was educated, fluent in German and well read. No one would deny her intelligence. She was also strident, opinionated, outspoken. And loud. Over the course of her lifetime, she would prove to be resilient.

On that day in Rotterdam, Midshipman Quinn made a beeline

Ruth Quinn's husband, then Navy Ensign Charles Henry Quinn, 1926. *Quinn family.*

for the two young women and introduced himself. Would they like to attend a dance on his ship that evening? All *aboveboard*, of course. If they did not mind the double entendre, the ladies were undoubtedly flattered to be pursued like this. It was a festive party held on the fantail of his ship on a warm, moonlit night. A flirtation between Midshipman Quinn and Miss Leyendecker ensued.

It was a long courtship—six years. Charles Quinn asked Ruth to marry him several times. She demurred. She apparently was not in a hurry to get married. As a daughter of affluence, she probably did not need a husband to provide her financial security. She seemed to enjoy her life in New York City, where she devoted considerable time to charity work, volunteering in hospitals with a group called the Almoners. They were the forerunners of social workers, identifying patients who needed subsidized care and organizing aftercare services.

An accomplished singer who loved the opera and the symphony, she frequently sang for society events. But the single life was frowned on in Ruth's devout Catholic family. Unless the daughters planned to enter the convent, they were expected to marry and have children. While Ruth was courted by many eligible bachelors of similar social status—including a member of the Mellon family in Pittsburgh—no one seemed to be as persistent as the suitor she had met in Rotterdam. When Charles Quinn asked Ruth one more time for her hand in marriage ("Ruth, either yes or no?"), she finally accepted.

She was thirty years old at the time of her wedding, a spinster by her generation's standards. In a reversal of tradition, several hundred guests attended a wedding reception the evening before the nuptials at the Hotel Barclay, which was hosted by Ruth's mother, Mrs. Leyendecker. Ruth and Charles were married the next morning on October 30, 1930, in St. Patrick's Cathedral. Immediately following, they headed to the pier to embark on a honeymoon cruise to California.

Like Ruth, Charles Quinn was born and raised in New York City. He, too, was Catholic and hailed from an immigrant family. But the Quinns were members of a different social class. Charles's father, Michael Joseph Quinn, was a "northern wetback," as his grandson Chuck called him, because he illegally immigrated from Ireland to the United States through Canada.

A New York City detective, Mike Quinn was appointed to the police force in 1892, serving for thirty-two years—including time in the Tenderloin district on the city's West Side. Six foot, two inches tall and weighing 240 pounds, he boasted an intimidating presence. He earned the nickname "Strong Arm Mike" for his forceful policing methods. Also a bootlegger and owner of a bar on the West Side of Manhattan, Mike Quinn was rumored to be in business with Sherman Billingsley, a notorious mobster and owner of the famous speakeasy the Stork Club.

He and his wife raised their thirteen children at 24 Audubon Avenue in the Bronx. Charles's mother was a Flanagan, of a family from Middletown, New York, that was associated with trotting horses and harness racing—either as trainers or owners, or both.

Humble origins notwithstanding, Charles took care and spent money to look sharp. His sister commented on his penchant for fastidiousness dating back to his youth. He took a taxicab home when it rained so as not to get his clothes wet. This would make him a suitable match for Ruth Leyendecker, who also was known for her tidiness.

Charles was religious and responsible. Attending to altar boy duties at church daily, he led the processions and, before his voice deepened, he sang the solo, the *Kyrie Eleison*, angelically. Charles was enthralled with the Order of the Passionist Fathers, a religious order of men who devote their life to preaching about Jesus around the world, missionaries of sorts.

Charles carved a heart out of wood and painted it black—in homage to the emblem of the Sacred Heart of Jesus, a symbol of the Passionists. He seriously considered joining the order, but his priest discouraged him from pursuing this interest, as he felt Charles was too young to make such a commitment.

Instead, Charles went to the Naval Academy and pursued a career in naval aviation. In this era, flying was the Wild West of the U.S. Navy. It was a career path pioneered by hardy, adventuresome men who tamed planes and dared to land them on the pitching deck of a ship, with a landing strip the length of three football fields.

After graduating from the Naval Academy and being commissioned an officer in 1926, Charles was selected to join this elite fraternity at Naval Air Station Pensacola in 1928. He entered flight school and successfully completed the rigorous training required to wear the "wings of gold" of a naval aviator, a feat accomplished by only a handful of men in the 1920s.

From Pensacola, Charles was assigned to VF Squadron 3-B on the aircraft carrier USS *Lexington* in San Diego. His early officer fitness reports described Charles as industrious and conscientious, level-headed, quiet, self-contained and conservative. In summary: "Well qualified for combat and carrier aviation duty." Other supervisors characterized him as careful, painstaking and—no surprise—very smart in appearance.

By the time Charles Quinn married Ruth Leyendecker in 1930, he was serving his second tour of duty as an aviator. Ruth and Charles visited Coronado after their honeymoon cruise down the Atlantic coast, through the Panama Canal and ending in California. It must have been her first exposure to the island *and* to the U.S. Navy.

Ruth had spent her entire life in Manhattan—except for her four years at Trinity College in Washington, D.C. Now, as a naval officer's wife, she was facing the unsettling prospect of moving every year or two. And as a naval *aviator's* wife, Ruth might have also felt uneasy about the dangers of Charles's chosen career path. But she was not allowed to show this discomfort.

These cultural attitudes were later codified in a popular guidebook for women who married naval officers. *The Navy Wife*, published in 1942, summarized the expectations for women like Ruth:

> *Even in times of peace there is an entirely different atmosphere in a regular naval air station from that in the average naval yard. There is an unspoken restraint—there is the ever-present dread of "Crash Signal"—accident and death. To keep the shadow in the background, there is a certain tenseness,*

an almost hysterical gaiety at times. There is also an esprit de corps that distinguishes these flying officers. They are welded together by the high and constant seriousness of their responsibility.

This career path attracted men with a lot of bravado—arguably necessary for their missions.

The Navy Wife's authors warned: "The high, emotional tension under which a flyer's wife lives will eventually break her unless she is made of pretty stern stuff." With the warnings came encouragement, too: "It gets into your blood, the men love to fly, and every wife is proud of her flying husband, his wings, and what they represent. It is a glorious life, fraught with danger but thrilling, devastating, and soul-satisfying."

Culturally, Ruth was no stranger to the social expectations of a Navy wife. She grew up in a family that took European vacations and formally entertained on a regular basis. Traveling to new places would not have been intimidating. After all, she was a Heide.

Navigating the maze of myriad formal social functions customarily held by and for naval officers and their wives also would not have felt unfamiliar or uncomfortable. And the ubiquitous cocktails at these social events probably did not faze her, either. The Navy took this habit to a whole new level: toasting with alcohol was an integral part of Navy social traditions, embedded in their rituals and expected of all Navy men.

So Ruth attended many social functions, large and small. She had no choice. Her husband's career depended on it. She could hold her own in a conversation about anything and expressed no reservations about offering her opinions on politics, business, opera and life in big cities like New York. She was erudite: university-educated, bilingual and extremely well-read and well-traveled. Indeed, she was much more worldly than most of the other young naval officers' wives with whom she was expected to socialize, most of whom were raised in middle-class households. At dinner parties, she could be quite the conversationalist. This skill sometimes did not work to her advantage: she had an annoying habit of talking while eating, causing her to project spittle and chewed morsels at her dinner companions.

The Navy's strict pecking order was probably annoying to someone who was raised at the top of New York society. Navy wives wore their husbands' ranks during this era, and she was married to a junior naval officer— meaning *she* was "ranked" toward the bottom of the social ladder. Ruth was also expected to show some deference to the wives of more senior officers. Indeed, on arriving at a new duty station, wives like Ruth Quinn were expected to pay social calls, in gloves and a hat, to their commanding officers and their families. Calling cards and knowing the rules of when to turn down the corner of a calling card—to indicate it had been delivered in person and *not* by a servant—were de rigueur. She may have chafed at these social customs.

A three-generational portrait of Ruth Leyendecker Quinn, Johanna Heide Leyendecker and newborn Charles Henry Quinn Jr., 1933. *Quinn family.*

Some in Navy society thought Ruth was haughty, rude, bombastic and weirdly loud. They said she badmouthed senior officers' wives, a major faux pas in this tribe. Her son simply said: "She was very cool to the Navy."

For the first three years of their marriage, Ruth found herself living in Hawaii, another island with an even more exotic and tropical environment. It was there that she and Charles celebrated Easter of 1933, in Pearl Harbor, with a new arrival: their firstborn son, Charles Henry Quinn Jr. Ruth's father, Dr. Leyendecker, was delighted when he received the news in a telegram. He responded with a whimsical note typed onto a calendar page dated April 10, 1933:

> *April 10: Birthday of Admiral Charles Henry Quinn, Jr. My dear Ruth, I am sure that calendars published about the year 2016 will bear the above reference. I received your or rather Charles Henry Quinn Jr.'s Easter Greeting yesterday noon after coming home from mass....It is a good thing that Charles Henry Quinn Jr., did not arrive today in New York. It has been "a nasty" Easter Sunday, and the only sunny day we have had thus far in April, was April 10th 1933, CHARLES HENRY QUINN's Birthday....Perhaps you will recollect the cry of the dying General at the Battle of Quebec: "They come! Let them Come!!! Mes amitiés à toute la Famille." Affectioneusement, Grandfather P.T.L.*

Dr. Leyendecker was somewhat prophetic: Charles Henry Quinn Jr. *would* live a very long life, long past 2016, but he would not become an admiral. Neither would his father, who would not even survive World War II.

5

MAMA'S BOY

My job is to take care of my mother.
—*Hank Leyendecker*

"Hi ho!" Ruth Quinn's baby brother Hank Leyendecker called as he waved while driving down Orange Avenue to head to the tennis courts at the Hotel del. Everyone knew Hank by his signature greeting and his car, which he named Lucinda. It was a black 1941 Ford coupe with Wyoming license plates, an "H" painted on the doors and a V-8 engine. The vehicle was an admired fixture around the island. No one was allowed to touch it.

Hank came to Coronado with his mother in 1937, when she moved to be closer to Ruth and her young family. He was Johanna's only son, and she was probably protective of him. Other than his stint at the prestigious boys' boarding school Georgetown Preparatory in Bethesda, Maryland, and Princeton University—where he attended but did not graduate—he did not veer far from Johanna for long.

Hank spent many of his days playing tennis, often on court #4 at the Hotel del. The resort maintained an oceanfront beach and tennis club available to island residents. Since its opening in 1889, the "Del"—as it is called in shorthand—served as the island's social center.

It was the largest resort hotel in the world at the time and, upon its opening in 1888, instantly became a major attraction for the wealthy leisure class of the twentieth century, a perfect place to escape the heat and humidity of East Coast summers. Some, like Hank and his mother, Johanna, made

Top: Hank Leyendecker's beloved 1941 Ford coupe he called "Lucinda." *Valerie Quate.*

Bottom: Hotel del Coronado promotional photo, 1948. *Coronado Historical Association Collection.*

it their year-round home. The Del became a playground for Hollywood's rising stars, including Mae West, Doris Day, Marilyn Monroe, Jack Lemmon, Tony Curtis, Anita Page, John Wayne and George Burns. The nascent film industry decided the island was an ideal location to film blockbusters like *Some Like It Hot, Wings Over the Navy* and *The Stunt Man.*

British royalty, especially those who served in the Royal Navy, were frequent visitors. Famously, Edward, Prince of Wales, was rumored to have wooed Wallis Simpson here, where she lived with her first husband, a naval aviator. Edward later abdicated the throne to marry Simpson. An author named Frank Baum spent his summers in a rental house just a stone's throw from the Hotel del. There, he wrote *The Wizard of Oz.* The book's images of the city of Oz look eerily like an emerald-green version of the Del.

At the Del's tennis club, Hank held court—pun intended. He was, by all accounts, an excellent tennis player—rated 4.5 or 5.0 by today's standards. For the courts, he tended to overdress and in multiple layers: he donned 1930s-era tennis shorts or long white pants. Tall, trim and aloof, he sized up his opponents with his piercing eyes. After a match, he piled on three sweaters and a blue blazer—with all the buttons askew and a towel wrapped around his neck like an ascot. Plagued with skin cancer from decades of sun worshipping with a metal reflector, his sharp and pointy facial features became garish later in life—scabbed, scarred and stretched from too many excisions and skin grafts. He covered his scarecrow look with big sunglasses and a mess of smelly, oily salves.

He was famous for his "Hankronysms," which he voiced loudly while he played. If the ball was out, he yelled: "OUT like Lottie's eye!" A double fault elicited, "The old base on ball." And a good shot earned you another: "Hi Ho!"

After each game, he told all the players, "It's in the book," referring to a journal he claimed to keep. In it, he said, he detailed the scores, significant rallies and his partner's skills—as well as *all* his own activities. Hank vowed *everything* he did or said or thought was in the book. It proved to be an idle threat, as this book of Hank's alleged activities was never found by the police, shedding no light on his sister's murder.

Until Johanna Leyendecker died in 1957, she rented adjoining rooms for her and Hank on the third floor of the Hotel del, overlooking the courtyard. There they lived for twenty years, taking all their meals in the dining room, regularly attending the dances and cocktail parties that were central to the island's social scene and hosting Ruth's family for lunch every Sunday after Mass—and for all family celebrations.

Hank Leyendecker was renowned for sunning on the beach, usually with a metal reflector. *Valerie Quate.*

And there, in Coronado, Hank *did* look after his mother. Without a husband in tow, a male sidekick in a world that still attempted to have equal numbers of men and women at parties was useful. Hank could serve in that role when needed. Like Ruth, he grew up attending high-society functions and knew how to comport himself with the high-ranking military officers, politicians, royalty and celebrities who frequented the Hotel del. Hank took his responsibilities to his mother seriously: he never held another paying job.

Johanna, while she did take care of Hank financially, never took care of him or his siblings emotionally. That role fell to Ruth.

Only five years older than Hank, she acted less like a sister and more like an overbearing, domineering mother figure—especially after Johanna died. Several evenings a week, Hank trotted over to Ruth's house for dinner. Ruth was a good cook, expertly trained at cooking school.

Ruth's son Chuck surmised: "She took care of him from the time that he was born because my grandma [Johanna] was a marvelous woman, but kind of impractical. The role of caring for the younger siblings fell in my mother's lap."

Hank and Ruth both loved and hated each other. They were codependent. Or at least *he* was dependent on *her*, and he apparently never outgrew this dependency. "It started when they were children," Chuck said. They clashed constantly, with Ruth's short temper flaring nightly.

Their conversation at dinner would frequently devolve into a shouting match in which Ruth demeaned Hank, criticized him, ridiculed him, belittled him. Neighbors could often hear the yelling and screaming. People around town felt sorry for him and the way she talked to him and about him.

Hank Leyendecker (*right*), in his usual tennis attire, poses for a photo in the 1970s, with Joe Ditler (*left*) and Hal Sweat after their weekly match. *Joe Ditler.*

Hank, wearing his friend's military cover, posing at a Hotel del party, circa 1950s. *Valerie Quate.*

Despite the ridicule and the outbursts, Hank never stormed out the door after eating. He stayed for a little after-dinner television. And then he spent the night in Ruth's second bedroom. Despite her visceral dislike of him, she continued to keep the door open for him. Hank never lost his cool with Ruth—as far as anyone knows.

In fact, no one who knew him well ever saw him lose his temper—not his tennis partners, not his nephew, not his companion of thirty years, not her children.

Lifelong bachelor Hank raised an eyebrow or two, a dandy living as he did with his mother and never marrying, but he did have a lady friend: Laura Christian. When he was not having dinner and spending the night with Ruth, he was eating dinner with Laura, who was alternatively described as his friend or his girlfriend. A twice-divorced single mother of two, she lived in a Tudor-style home at 1015 Encino Row on the island, a block from the beach. The two probably met at the Hotel del.

Hank called her "Little Laura," because she was only about five foot, three inches, much shorter than Hank. The daughter and daughter-in-law of Navy admirals, she settled in Coronado and raised her two children there. She was strikingly pretty, with a resemblance to Ingrid Bergman. Despite her status as a divorcée, which carried a stigma in that era, she was a catch.

"He was really sweet to her," Laura's daughter Valerie Quate remembered. Though many might have whispered about Hank's strange lifestyle and proclivities, Valerie insisted Hank and Laura's relationship was a romantic one. But it was quirky: Laura frequently joked that Hank loved Lucinda—

Top: Hank Leyendecker and Laura Christian (*front row, far left*) at a dinner party at the Hotel del with Liberace (*seated far right*), circa 1950s. *Valerie Quate.*

Bottom: Hank Leyendecker and his companion of thirty years, Laura Christian. *Valerie Quate.*

his car—more than he loved her. And they never married. Perhaps it was because they were both Catholic and Laura was divorced. Yet even after her first husband died, freeing her to marry (in the eyes of the Catholic church), they never tied the knot. Nor they did live together; their generation probably would not have considered such an unorthodox arrangement.

After Hank's mother died, he moved out of the Hotel del and into a room that he rented from a retired couple, Jas and Rhea Miller, at 732 B Avenue. He kept the room for twenty years, even though he slept in Ruth's second bedroom almost every night.

Hank's constant presence in her home annoyed Ruth. In a letter she wrote to her son in 1965, she complained about it: "Right from the start I made it clear that as long as I lived that was your room—and should you ever want it, Hank would automatically return to the Millers. It would strike me as ridiculous that you rent a room at a motel [when you visit], while he is in your room—and his room at the Millers' is empty."

It *was* odd that Hank would pay his own money to rent space that he rarely used for twenty years. Hank was notoriously cheap. He frequently ate at the cafeteria at the Coronado Hospital. When he sat at the counter for breakfast at Clayton's, the island diner, he brought his own grapefruit and used the free salt and sugar. When he took Laura out to dinner, he never paid for drinks—preferring to bring his own and drink in the car. He rarely left a tip. When he gave gifts to Laura's children, they were boxes of Jujubes and Jujyfruits.

However, Hank's image of himself did not include "cheapskate." In addition to dressing for tennis like a swell, Hank often sported a belt with a big shiny buckle, calling himself a cowboy. His nephew Chuck was convinced he *was* one because Hank had spent so much time on

Hank Leyendecker rented a room for more than twenty years from the Millers, who owned this house at 732 B Avenue, a block from Sacred Heart Church. *Author's collection.*

56

Hank Leyendecker at Eatons' Ranch in Wolf, Wyoming. *Valerie Quate.*

a cattle ranch in Wyoming called Eatons'. Hank's nickname was the "Manhattan Cowboy."

Hank was most likely first sent there as a kid because spending time outdoors would have been good for his constitution. He had been a sickly, asthmatic youth and frequently described as fragile. Dr. and Mrs. Leyendecker probably thought the air in Wyoming would be better than in Manhattan, and perhaps Hank could gain some physical strength and male hardiness from exposure to ranch life.

Eatons' Ranch was not a commercial cattle ranch. It was a dude ranch, the oldest one in the country. Dude ranches were so-called because they hosted "dudes"—houseguests from the East Coast who had their own ideas of "correct" western dress and who paid for their extended stays. Working cowboys on the ranch found the dudes amusing, with their "immense hats, big revolvers, rattlesnake belts and leather 'chaps.'" At some point in the late 1800s, the Eaton family realized that the dude business was more profitable than the cattle business. The dude ranch was born, and the Eatons hosted the sons of wealthy families like the Heides and the Roosevelts, as well as generals like George C. Marshall and celebrities like Cary Grant.

As the Eatons recounted in a 1910 magazine article:

> *An old friend asked him, as a personal favor, to take charge of his younger son, a wayward youth, in the hope that in the West, away from metropolitan temptations, he might make a man of himself. Eaton readily agreed. This gave him an idea as to the possibilities of the dude traffic.... The young men looked upon it as a great lark and came west in droves.*

Hank, one of Eatons' longtime dudes, loved the experience and returned often. He and the other guests learned how to ride horses and went on roundups. They hunted antelopes and prairie chickens. They camped and fought grass fires. And they pretended to be cowboys. Like many other dudes, Hank got the costume right: he wore a cowboy hat, dusty jeans, fringed leather chaps, cowboy boots and that big shiny silver belt buckle. It was decorated with a longhorn with ruby eyes, one of Hank's favorite personal possessions, which his nephew Chuck coveted all his life. And it was here at Eatons' where Hank is said to have retreated during World War II. Unlike his brother-in-law and most adult men of his generation, sickly Hank Leyendecker never served in the military.

Hank spent part of every year and some of his happiest days at Eatons' Ranch. In the summer of 1939, however, the outdoor life was not agreeing with him. He was severely depressed. Ruth received two letters of appeal from a doctor and his wife in Sheridan, Wyoming: "We are really concerned about Hank. He's not responding at all. We have moved him in with us six weeks ago. Won't you please come and see what you can do?"

As always, Ruth felt responsible for Hank. She determined she needed to travel to Eatons' Ranch to check on him. It was a place she had not visited since 1930. Against her husband's wishes, Ruth rushed to Hank's aid in Wyoming. She left her two young sons, six-year-old Chuck and three-year-old Michael, in the care of a babysitter, a decision that marked her for the rest of her life.

6

A TRUCK TURNS THE BEND

I want you to be a very good boy—remember you are the man of the house and you must take good care of Mommy and your brother Michael who really likes you.
—Letter from Lieutenant Commander Charles Quinn to Chuck, spring 1939

Chuck heard the screeching of brakes ahead. Straining to peer down the street, he saw a dump truck swerve in the road, heard a thump and made out a limp figure being hurled backward through the air. "My first thought was that it was the big, mean Doberman Pinscher that belonged to our neighbors, the Tarbucks."

Six years old, Chuck had been sitting on the back end of his friend's bicycle, his arms wrapped around her waist, as she pedaled. He jumped off the bike and ran toward the scene of the accident and the lump by the side of the road.

It was a warm morning in July 1939. All the children living in Coronado were out of school for summer vacation, and they were spending all day every day outside. They tossed marbles in the dirt, raced their Flexi-Flyers, chased one another in games of cowboys and Indians, hopscotched and rode bicycles and tricycles up and down the sidewalks.

Ruth was out of town, tending to Hank, who was in a deep depressive state at the Eatons' dude ranch in Wyoming. Chuck had heard his father admonish Ruth not to go out of town: "VF-3 has its hands full: long hours, fleet testing, a new plane. *Don't go.* I'm flying all the time and Michael and Chuck need you." But Ruth apparently believed that Hank needed her more.

War would not break out in Europe until the end of that summer, when Hitler invaded Poland on September 1. American leaders knew Germany and Hitler were threats. But isolationism still dominated national politics and popular sentiment. War had not yet affected the military families living in Coronado. And the island always felt like a refuge. "We were safe there," Dick Tarbuck remembered.

But the military knew war was coming, and Navy leaders were quickly trying to increase their capacity—of planes, aircraft carriers and pilots. Training time was cut in half from one year to six months. Chuck's father was serving as the executive officer of VF-3 at nearby Naval Air Station North Island. Known for the "Felix the Cat" insignia on their planes, this squadron's pilots flew the Grumman F3F-1, at the time a new biplane fighter aircraft built for the Navy. As the second-in-command of VF-3, Lieutenant Commander Quinn had a significant amount of responsibility.

At the time, the Quinns lived just two houses from the corner of Fifth Street and Pomona Avenue. In 1939, Pomona was a wide and busy street,

Six-year-old Chuck Quinn and his brother, three-year-old Michael, swimming in the Hotel del Coronado pool in 1939, the summer Michael was hit and killed by a truck. *Quinn family.*

the major supply route between NAS North Island and the Silver Strand highway, the only land route to San Diego at the time. It was also a curvy street, with blind spots for its steady stream of traffic.

When Chuck heard the thud and saw the little body arcing through the air, he ran to see who it was. "There on the opposite corner, lying on his back next to the curbstone on the grass was the little body of my dear brother, Michael. His shirt was torn on his chest and there was blood on his head and face."

"Come on over to see my shiny new red tricycle," Michael's friend had called out from across the street.

Though he had been told not to cross busy Pomona Avenue, the three-year-old toddler must have been enticed by the shiny object—and oblivious to the oncoming traffic. Fixated on the tricycle, little Michael darted between the parked cars lining Pomona Avenue and ran into the street just as the dump truck was rounding a bend in the road.

Chuck reminisced: "Michael was a very good boy. In fact, he was like an angel. Everyone loved him." Chuck always felt that little Michael was the favored child. "He knew he was not allowed to cross the street. But his age of three-and-a-half and the sight of the new tricycle caused him to lose his awareness in the moment."

The dump truck's driver never saw Michael, hidden by the parked cars on the right side of the street. Michael hurtled into the side of the truck. He suffered a fractured skull and a broken arm and died almost instantly. "Even if Michael had looked, he may not have been able to see the truck coming because of the curve of the avenue."

The shaken truck driver emerged from behind the wheel. Adults from around the neighborhood ran to the scene. Mrs. Tarbuck gently grabbed Chuck and her son Dick by the arms, guiding them inside her house and away from the tragic scene.

To take their minds off the trauma the two boys had just witnessed, "Dick and I were invited to spend the rest of the day aboard his father's ship," Chuck remembered. Dick's dad was in command of the destroyer USS *McDonough*, moored in the San Diego Harbor. He invited the boys to take the captain's launch from the dock to the ship, where they were treated to lunch in the wardroom and a tour.

Ruth rushed home from Wyoming, leaving the bedside of her depressed brother to tend to her traumatized husband and son in Coronado. A few mornings after the tragedy, as the Quinn family prepared to bury little Michael, the doorbell rang. There on the doorstep stood the truck driver, in tears. Ruth invited him inside to the living room and served him a cup of coffee. Amid sobs, he said that Michael had just run out from behind a parked car right into the side of his truck. He never saw the little boy. He begged the Quinns for forgiveness. Ruth consoled him, Chuck remembered. "She was able to make him feel a little better that morning."

Chuck's father blamed Ruth for not being home. Ruth probably resented her husband for blaming her and most likely harbored some ill will toward Hank for taking her away from her family. She also must have felt some guilt for not being home.

Like his father, Chuck blamed his mother for not being there to protect Michael. At the end of his life, Chuck claimed that Ruth blamed him for not watching out for his little brother.

What a heavy weight to carry.

The trauma created a lifetime of tension, which triggered volatile outbursts from everyone in the family and a lot of drinking. As Chuck said at the end of his life, "It ruined a lot of lives that day."

7
DEATH IN BROOKLYN

Should have been with us for our 13th skunk. Although we are proud of new war valor we will miss our friends in the Atlantic. Best luck and regards. Dufek and Quinn.
—Message from USS Bogue *executive officer Commander Charles Quinn and his commanding officer to the battleship USS* Wyoming, *after sinking their thirteenth German U-boat in the Battle of the Atlantic, June 1945*

C ome on, Chuck." His father held out his hand. The two were exploring a cave together. It was one of the last father-son outings Chuck Quinn remembered before his father deployed to World War II and made history in the Battle of the Atlantic. He never saw him again.

At the end of Chuck's life, when his memory was failing, his recollection of this adventure he took with his dad was still sharp. He could recite all the details.

Entering the yawning cave in La Jolla, California, Chuck felt very small. It was pitch black inside the mouth, the waves sloshing in and out. "I had to walk across the stones barefoot," he remembered. Taking a deep breath, he stepped tentatively, trying to balance himself and get a grip on the slippery rocks, and reached toward his father's outstretched hand. He made it and grabbed it. Together, they explored. He felt secure, tethered.

This was rare. Chuck's father was never at home, and Chuck was always left alone with his mother. From Chuck's birth until his father died twelve years later, Commander Charles Quinn was always absent—deployed at sea and at war.

He was trying to climb the ladder of the officer corps and prove his mettle as a combat pilot. In his frequent absences, his dad used handwritten letters to Chuck to impart fatherly discipline, guidance, concern and love. When he died suddenly, far away from home, all Chuck had left was the letters—sixteen of them. Chuck kept each one, rereading and annotating them over the course of his very long life.

In one of the earliest cards to "Charlie," Charles sent birthday greetings from afar:

> *Dear Charlie Boy,*
> *At the time of your second birthday I will be at sea. I regret that I will be unable to spend that particular day with you. But your dear mother will be there—and I will be thinking of you and wishing you a happy time—with all the nice things that mother plans for you. Be a good fellow and I will look forward to being with you as soon as time permits—Happy Birthday. Your loving father, DaDa.*
> *—On board my boat, the cruiser USS* Astoria, *Long Beach, California, April 7, 1935*

The future had looked prosperous for Charles Quinn back in 1935. Though the nation was still immersed in the funk of the Great Depression, those men serving in the military during this interwar period were enjoying relative economic stability. Charles was also living in heady times: naval aviators were daring, pushing the limits of their planes and trying to demonstrate their ability to be more than scouts for the Navy's battleships and cruisers.

The community of naval aviators was still the realm of a small and exclusive club, mostly composed of "ring knockers"—graduates of the U.S. Naval Academy. Charles was a member of that club. And he trained and served with many names who eventually made history in World War II. He was Joe Kennedy's flight instructor, and among his peers and personal friends were Butch O'Hare, the Navy fighter ace who was later killed in action (and was the namesake for the new airport in Chicago); Jimmie Thach, the brilliant air-to-air combat tactician who pioneered the evasive tactic known as the Thach Weave; and Jim Flatley—known as the "Reaper Leader" and the scion of the large Flatley family of naval officers, a fighter pilot who proved the superiority of the F4F Wildcat and later initiated major changes across all of naval aviation. Surely, Charles Quinn's career would ascend to similar heights.

With Charles absent from home much of his career, he could not be present with his family to serve as a physical role model for Chuck. Letters would have to suffice.

Just six months before little Michael's tragic death, Charles tried to impart a lesson in how to be a good big brother and not a bully:

Dear Chuck,

Mother wrote me about the very unfortunate accident that occurred to Michael. I am sure that his eye will be alright and that you will take care of him and see that his eye gets better. You are a good boy Chuck and I know that you did not mean to hurt your brother. Michael is a good little fellow and I know that he is deserving of your friendship....Much more so than the big boy that you were going to hit with that stick....I do not know who the boy is that you were fighting with. I am very glad that you did not hurt him—his mommy would have cried too—and we would have all been very

A rare photo of Chuck Quinn with *both* of his parents, Lieutenant Commander Charles Quinn (*left*) and Ruth Quinn, at the dedication of the St. Edwards Catholic Chapel at Naval Air Station Jacksonville, Florida, 1943. *U.S. Navy.*

sad. I know you did not mean to hurt him nor your brother Michael—but sticks and rocks do hurt and if you want to see, try it yourself. I'm sure Michael's eye will be alright—so do not worry. But let it be a lesson to play with boys your own size. You can help Michael to grow up—and then never pick up rocks or stones to fight with....
—*From United States Fleet Aircraft, Battle Force Fighting Squadron Three, aboard the aircraft carrier USS* Lexington, *January 17, 1939*

Little Michael was killed six months later. Chuck was the only family member at home at the time. Ruth was in Wyoming, at Eatons' Ranch, tending to Hank and his bout with depression. Charles was flying. His dad had told this six-year-old child that he was the "man of the house." The babysitter who was left in charge of the two boys became an alcoholic. Chuck would become one, too. Some of his father's colleagues said Commander Quinn turned to the bottle as well.

But Charles Quinn's work continued to keep him away from home. Ruth and Chuck were on their own to heal from the trauma of losing Michael.

In April 1940, Charles was serving on another aircraft carrier, USS *Saratoga.* For the next two years, Charles and his peers honed their antiaircraft bombing techniques and developed the first monoplane for the U.S. Navy, the Brewster F2A-1.

In another letter to Chuck, he described an unusual scene at sea, a "searchlight display," where more than three hundred ships turned on their searchlights at the same time. The light show against the Hawaiian skies "was very pretty and I am sure that the people in Honolulu enjoyed it." He included a drawing of his ship with its searchlights depicted like sun rays. In the letter, he predicted,

I expect to be home for your first communion day so be a good boy and learn your prayers and help mother. But above all, have a good time and a lot of fun. A big kiss for you and Mother. Your Daddy.
—*Afloat on USS* Saratoga, *April 25, 1940*

Promises made but not kept.

Dear Chuck, I want to congratulate you on making your first Holy Communion. I am very glad and very proud of you. Later on when you grow up to be a big man you will still be happy about your Communion Day. Keep it up!...I miss you very much. I hope I will be home with

you soon again. Be a good boy and take care of Mother for me. Love, Your Daddy
—From Lahaina Territory of Hawaii aboard USS Saratoga, *May 19, 1940*

Though he told Chuck he wanted to come home, instead Charles requested an extension of his sea duty assignment. He knew that being in a combat command would better serve his prospects for promotion—especially if the United States entered the war raging in Europe. His request was denied. When Pearl Harbor was attacked and President Franklin Roosevelt declared war in December 1941, Charles found himself out of the action, at a training command in Jacksonville, Florida, where he was initially passed over for promotion to commander. Making an appeal directly to Chief of Naval Operations Admiral Ernest J. King, he asked for reconsideration, citing his many accomplishments and dedication to the service.

Admiral King apparently agreed, because Charles was assigned to the carrier escort USS *Bogue.* And his fortunes changed.

The flagship of the Second Barrier Force, USS *Bogue* was commanded by his Naval Academy friend Captain George J. Dufek. Charles served as his air officer and, later, executive officer. With its accompanying destroyers, *Bogue* took on an antisubmarine mission. They were on the hunt for German U-boats, the submarines that had been decimating merchant vessels in the Atlantic. In 1942 alone, some 1,100 American merchant vessels were sunk—killing thousands of Americans and devastating supply lines.

The Allies first deployed land-based planes to ferret out the U-boats and sink them when they surfaced. But when the packs of U-boats clustered in the middle of the Atlantic, outside the range of those planes, merchant vessels were still vulnerable.

Bogue was deployed to test out a new tactic. "We got the *Bogue* and rushed it out on an experimental basis," said Admiral Walter K. "Killy" Kilpatrick, chief of staff of the Atlantic Fleet, in an interview with *Reader's Digest* in 1945.

Bogue and its squadrons of carrier-based fighter planes took over where the land-based planes could not—outside their range. "A complicated timetable—well, I guess it was the most complicated and finely drawn timetable ever made—took care of the speed problem eventually," Admiral Kilpatrick explained. "There should have been escort ships to protect the carrier, but we didn't have the escort ships and we couldn't wait for them. The war was slipping out of our grasp. So we just had to cross our fingers, and you can imagine how the Fleet felt when the *Bogue* sailed on its first mission. And how the men on the *Bogue* felt."

Bogue sank eleven German and two Japanese submarines. They were the last enemy submarines sunk in the Atlantic theater. Charles was promoted to commander and was awarded

Carrier escort USS *Bogue* underway, June 1944. *Destroyer Escort Historical Museum.*

a Bronze Star. The entire ship's crew received a Presidential Unit Citation for their role in finally vanquishing the U-boat menace. Both were high awards, and Commander Quinn's accomplishments made the newspapers back home in Coronado, no doubt instilling pride in Ruth and Chuck.

It was a triumphant end to the Battle of the Atlantic. Now that Charles had made history there and Germany had surrendered, *Bogue* and its flotilla of destroyers were going to enjoy the spoils of victory. Charles boarded a captured German submarine, locked up the German crew and sailed the sub into port in New York City. It was a triumphant return home for Commander Quinn.

Bogue was then headed to the Pacific theater to finish off the Japanese, and Charles was set to receive a command of his own.

In his last letter to Chuck on May 23, he offered more advice and discouraged his son from expecting a visit anytime soon. The war in Europe was over, but the Japanese were still in the fight: "I think you should go to camp as soon as you can and not waste

"This paper bird was sent to me by my father from an aircraft carrier he was aboard at the time. The tail is marked 'FB-1-C,' which was a U.S. Navy fighter bomber of the early '30s. It was a gift he would have sent me in one of the last two or three letters." *Quinn family.*

the summer waiting for me—At present, our plans are not too definite as to the exact time we will leave here for the West Coast."

Bogue pulled into port in the Brooklyn Navy Yard for repairs, in preparation for its passage through the Panama Canal en route to San Diego and then to finish off the Japanese in the Pacific.

While in port, Commander Quinn, forty-one, seemingly in the best of health, suddenly was not.

"Western Union—June 18, 1945—New York, NY—8:06 p.m.: Dear Ruth, I am very sorry to inform you that Charles is seriously ill with pneumonia in U.S. naval hospital St. Alban's Long Island, New York. Suggest you call Mae [Quinn] Galloway at midnight New York time tonight. Best regards to you and Chuck. George Dufek."

Pneumonia. It was a surprise to Captain Dufek, who claimed that Charles seemed to come down with the illness quite suddenly. He was placed under an oxygen tent and given penicillin. Out of the blue, he was fighting for his life. But according to Captain Dufek, "It looked for a while that he had an even chance."

Eighteen hours later, Commander Charles Quinn was dead.

He died just a few miles from where he was born. Ruth and Chuck buried him just a few feet away from little Michael.

A few weeks later, when *Bogue* pulled into port in San Diego, Captain Dufek invited Ruth and Chuck aboard. While "Uncle George" had a private meeting with Ruth, a crewman gave Chuck a tour of the ship, where he retraced the steps his father had made so many times over so many months at sea. Chuck touched the five-inch gun mounted on the stern, walked through the Combat Information Center, the bridge, the hangar deck where planes were normally tied down and finally to the flight deck. The crew was working on the

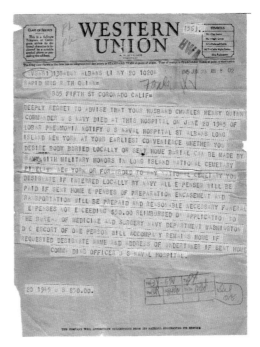

The telegram informing Ruth of her husband's sudden death from pneumonia, June 20, 1945. *Quinn family.*

69

catapult, the mechanism that shot planes off the deck of the ship. In Chuck's honor, the crew held a special ceremony for him: a block of solid wood was catapulted into the bay, arcing through the air before landing in the water with a large splash. The crew gave him a clip of 40mm antiaircraft shells as a war souvenir.

Chuck turned melancholy when he visited his father's small, cozy sea cabin. There was his rack, where he undoubtedly took ill. "On his desk there was a fine 8 in. x 10 in. photograph of me in a tan camel's hair sport jacket, and white shirt and tie."

Chuck Quinn, age eleven. *Quinn family.*

Navy wives expect to raise children on their own for months or years, and families expect months or years without their father. They brace themselves for combat casualties—but pneumonia?

Chuck spent his lifetime poring over the sixteen letters he received from his father, a man he barely knew, searching for clues to Commander Quinn's character. With few memories of his own, the letters were all he had. Yet Chuck was insistent: "My father was the greatest man I have ever known."

8

SPIRITUAL GUIDANCE

Spin carefully, not fearfully; Though wearily you plod. Spin carefully, spin prayerfully; But leave the thread to God.
—*Note to Ruth Quinn from Mother Genevieve Clarke, July 11, 1967*

I t was part of a birthday message to Ruth on her sixty-seventh birthday, written in Mother Genevieve Clarke's distinctively clean, tiny cursive handwriting that was embellished with little fountain pen flourishes:

> *I thank you for a dear and precious friendship which is the more appreciated as I know old age offers little of interest to keep the loyalty of friendship alive—and yet you have never changed—Gracias amiga. So, whatever that thing I am wishing you, is—the "best ever"—and (together) it will reach you "on the wings" of a day of prayer July eleventh, 1967. Love, G. Clarke*

Some twenty years older than Ruth, Mother Clarke had served for several decades as a confidante, spiritual mentor and surrogate big sister to Ruth. She was a member of the RSCJ, the same religious order that had educated Ruth in Albany, New York.

They had met when Ruth needed a job after Charles's death in 1945. Although she received a modest widow's benefit, it was not enough to make ends meet. She would not receive her Heide Company inheritance until her mother died. And that would not happen until 1957. She needed to support

Left to right: Reverend Mother Genevieve Clarke, Reverend Mother Rosalie Hill and Reverend Mother Suzanne de Leon in one of the San Diego College for Women patios in February 1957 during Mother Hill's Golden Jubilee celebration. *University of San Diego Archives.*

herself and her son Chuck. He would be ready for high school soon, and she wanted to send him to a Catholic boarding school.

This did not go over well with Chuck. He wanted to stay with his friends in Coronado and attend Coronado High School. His childhood friend John Elwell said this created a significant amount of ill will: "I mean his mother was very cruel to him and very demanding, made decisions in his life."

But her decision reigned. In 1947, when Chuck left for Ojai, California, to attend the all-boys Villanova Preparatory School, Ruth also left the island. She moved to San Francisco, where she spent a year in the Graduate School of Library Science at the University of California at Berkeley in hopes of working at a new college, the San Diego College for Women, that would be established in 1948 on a windswept hill near Old Town San Diego called Alcalá Park. Her studies were sponsored by another RSCJ nun named Mother Rosalie Hill. Mother Hill became the first president of the college, which opened to students in 1952. She wanted Ruth to set up the college's library.

When Ruth returned to San Diego with a degree in library science in hand, she instead went to work for the City of San Diego libraries, but she volunteered nights and weekends at San Diego College for Women with Mother Genevieve Clarke. Together, they organized and catalogued the new library's book collection.

The library received gifts from Catholics from all over the world: statues and figurines of the Madonna; hand-carved miniature Spanish Renaissance–style furniture, enough to fill a dollhouse; first editions of children's books by Beatrix Potter and a Latin version of *Winnie the Pooh*; remnants of a book collection rescued from the Barcelona Cathedral during the Spanish Civil War; a collection of signatures of U.S. presidents; Egyptian wall hangings; and the most valuable item, *The Book of Hours*, a rare volume of devotionals prepared by monks and printed before 1501.

For librarians and researchers, evaluating and archiving these treasures and developing displays for them would have been salivating. Working so closely together surrounded by stacks and books and card catalogues over many evenings and weekends undoubtedly drew Mother Clarke and Ruth closer together. Ruth did not seem to have any interest in dating or remarrying. And of course, Mother Clarke was celibate. The two most likely bonded over their shared isolation as single women who loved books.

They had much more in common. Mother Clarke was also born into affluence. Her father had made a fortune in the Klondike gold rush, and she had studied abroad in her youth. She aspired to become an opera singer but instead became a nun in 1904. Ruth loved opera.

Even after Ruth left and took a job at the Coronado Library, she and Mother Clarke remained the closest of friends and confidantes. Whenever Ruth's relationship with her son Chuck became unbearable—and that was often—Mother Clarke was the soothing salve between them. She was the only person who could reason with Chuck. She was the only one who could effectively hold him accountable for his behavior. She knew all his secrets.

9

TRYING TO FLY

I have an awful power. It destroys those whom I love. And this includes me.
—*Chuck Quinn in a letter to Mother Genevieve Clarke, August 19, 1959*

Shimmying up the ladder of the high dive at the Naval Air Station North Island Officers Club, Chuck stripped off his bathing suit and plunged into the pool. The wake from his cannonball soaked everyone on the pool deck. Then, in a flash, Chuck emerged, his nude body all shiny and wet and tan. Flashing his toothy grin, he started running. Six feet and 170 pounds, Chuck was lean and muscular with undulating waves of sun-bleached blond hair and a slow smile. And he was fast. A football player in high school and college, Chuck could outrun most men his age.

He sprinted into the parking lot, down the long driveway and toward the beach, Navy shore patrol in hot pursuit. Chuck left them in the dust. Like a sandpiper, he hopped across the dunes effortlessly and then dove into the ocean. A lithe swimmer and surfer at home in the water, Chuck disappeared into the waves.

It was the summer of 1956 or 1957, and Chuck was now a college graduate and twenty-three or twenty-four years old. He and several other Navy juniors, all of whom were lifeguards at Central Beach in Coronado, were attending a luau at the Officers' Club on a hill overlooking the ocean. The party was a good one, lasting late into the night.

Was drinking involved? "Yeah, he was drunk," his childhood friend Dr. Vince Flynn remembered. "He was such a good athlete, though, that he could pull that off without any problem." When Chuck drank, however, he drank a lot. In fact, he had already been arrested three times for drunkenness.

John Elwell, a fellow surfer who had known Chuck since age twelve, was a good friend of Chuck's for most of their lives. Like Chuck, John was a good surfer, but he was burlier, with bushy eyebrows and a moustache and more of a football player's build than Chuck. John summed up Chuck like this: "His life is a classic tale amongst surfers in my generation. He [was] smart, well educated, from a wealthy family, was a fine surfer and athlete, and [was] crazy."

He had company. Young men like John and Chuck who started surfing in the 1950s were in the vanguard of a sport that came to be synonymous with California culture. And they took significant risks with this hobby. By the early 1960s, around the same time the Beat generation was influencing San Francisco clubs and cafés, surfers were crowding the beaches of Southern California, testing the limits with their boards on increasingly large waves.

When Gidget surf movies hit the theaters and the Beach Boys dominated the airwaves with surfer music, the sport went commercial and the craze became a national one. The boys who were good at surfing became more popular with the teenage girls than the football players were.

At twenty-three, Chuck was Hollywood handsome and a natural athlete, earning mild celebrity status in surfing.

He conquered the waves at Windansea in La Jolla and the Tijuana Sloughs. At Big Waimea, he dared to ride in a perfect Tom Blake–style pose through the dangerous barrel. John said he is on record with pioneering surfing filmmaker Bud Browne as getting the longest ride ever filmed at Mākaha, Hawaii—a length that has allegedly never been equaled. Chuck says this legendary ride is documented in Browne's film *Gun Ho!*.

But he was just as good on the slopes. And his skiing exploits landed him in a two-page photo spread in a 1959 issue of *National Geographic*. The article described the fervor for the winter sport that was fast becoming a popular pastime for Americans, chronicling its explosive growth: four hundred ski areas had developed in twenty-eight states in twenty years. The article's photographer captured Chuck in a bright red sweater "skimming the heights" in the mountains of Alta, Utah—his favorite place to ski and where he spent ten winters working ski patrol and as an instructor. Skiing also took him to Sun Valley, Idaho; Lake Tahoe, California; and Jackson Hole, Wyoming.

Above: Chuck "Gunker" Quinn from Coronado bringing his Bob Simmons surfboard to the Tijuana Sloughs, 1952. *John Elwell.*

Right: Chuck Quinn earned the lifelong nickname "Gunker" when he was a Coronado lifeguard. *John Elwell.*

Aspiring to be an aviator like his father, he had entered Air Force ROTC in college. But the military required aviators to have uncorrected 20/20 vision, and Chuck did not have perfect eyesight. So, Chuck said, "I wore contact lenses when I was taking the examinations." This was not allowed. He was caught, which must have horrified his mother, who was a stickler for the truth.

He was kicked out of the ROTC program, his chance at becoming an officer dashed.

Instead, he enlisted in the Navy and served as a dental technician in San Diego while living at home in Coronado with Ruth. That service lasted only two years and was marked by frequent incidents of missing muster and showing up late. He also had a habit of getting into arguments with his peers and supervisors. Over the course of his life, Chuck would

On Wings of Wood, an Expert Skims the Heights Above Alta

Chuck Quinn in Alta, Utah, in a photo spread and article on skiing in *National Geographic*, February 1959. *Kathleen Revis for National Geographic.*

work as a marine carpenter, retail salesman, longshoreman, phone company customer service rep, medical research assistant, postal clerk and veterinary technician. His job there was to euthanize animals.

Most of these stints were short-lived. The jobs Chuck held the longest were those that tapped into his athletic prowess: ski instructor and Coronado lifeguard. But even those employments were challenging. According to John Elwell, Chuck was not a reliable lifeguard. He was irresponsible, frequently reporting to work late and hungover. John and the other lifeguards often had to let him sleep off the hangover for a couple of hours. Chuck also had a habit of going to the bathroom in the ocean, earning him a lifelong nickname: the Gunker.

With his good looks and athletic prowess, Gunker impressed the ladies, and he took advantage of their interest, becoming quite the lothario and leaving a trail of broken hearts. He conceived two children with two different women. He raised neither and barely knew either one.

The closest he came to marriage was to the Southern California real estate heiress Joan Irvine, whose family owned and developed massive swaths of Orange County farmland. Chuck and Joan met in Ensenada, Mexico, at a yacht race. The attraction was instant and electric. Chuck whisked her off to Catalina Island for a weekend of sailing and lovemaking.

Joan was down-to-earth and pretty with a square, freckled face and kind blue eyes. She was an avid horseback rider and wore her hair in a long braid down her back. A minority shareholder of the Irvine Company, she was already serving on its board of directors when she met Chuck.

For Joan, it was "the summer that never ended." For Chuck, it was the love of a lifetime. Sixty years later, he claimed, "I love her as much today as I did then." Chuck wanted to marry her, but Ruth did not approve. Joan was divorced (and the mother of two children), and the Quinns were devout Catholics. The engagement was called off. In hindsight, he said, somewhat defensively, "She was not one for the marrying life."

It was around this time that Gunker had his first serious mental breakdown. Unfortunately for Ruth, who was called to bail him out of difficult circumstances, this breakdown took place in Tahiti, making the bailout particularly expensive.

Tahiti: a place where men have gone for generations to experience an exotic tropical paradise and to seduce barely clad *vahines*, the term for the local sirens. There was a sense of freedom on this mythical island— freedom from Western rules and standards and morals, freedom from societal obligations. The artist Paul Gauguin famously left his wife and children to indulge in this Tahitian style of liberty. In 1959, jet service was not yet serving Tahiti. It was not overrun with tourists as Hawaii was. The largest town on the island was Papeete, where half the population lived, and the most notorious bar in town was called, coincidentally, Quinn's.

Despondent over the breakup with Joan, Chuck jumped at the chance to join his childhood friend Ted Johnson on an extended trip to Tahiti. Ski season was over, and Chuck had no job for the summer. It was an offer he could not pass up.

Arriving by ship, Chuck was intoxicated by the colors, the music and the women—some of the most beautiful in the world, he thought. "It really is carefree," he wrote in a letter to a friend in early August. "You can talk to whoever you please—and get up and leave whenever you want and do what you want—Nobody cares—and most people don't even bother to look. They don't think you're an oddball just because you don't conform."

He stayed in an old hotel that doubled as a bordello. Paul Gauguin's son, who made money getting his picture taken with tourists, lived next door. Chuck spent much of his time for the first few weeks exploring the town of Papeete and some of the neighboring islands, writing and taking photographs. He entertained the idea of publishing a book of his photographs and musings. He sent Ruth a laundry list of items to ship to him ("orders," she called them). Included in the list, of course, was a request for money.

Ruth's response was polite but firm: "I inherited a modest amount from Mother, almost all of it in securities, which will give me an income equivalent to my former salary." Ruth had retired that summer from her last librarian job at the Coronado Public Library.

Chuck Quinn in front of Quinn's bar in Papeete, Tahiti, summer 1959. Back of photo: "Remember the old white-haired lady that sold flower hats in Quinn's. She is sitting there with me." *Quinn family.*

I will be happy to help you out up to a point, but paying me back at some vague future date will not pay my bills now. And surely, I cannot sell my securities to keep you in Tahiti indefinitely. No doubt I can arrange for a modest monthly allowance, and at any time you are ready to come home, I will be happy to pay your way back. But I really feel that if you cannot afford to stay in Tahiti, you should come back and take a job and support yourself, and do your writing and photography in your spare time.

Chuck probably knew that he would have to leave when his stash of cash ran out. And he wanted to stay. The pressure and, maybe, a venereal disease got to him. He stayed awake for days, drinking. He became agitated and aggressive. His friend Ted said he could not control Chuck and barely was able to prevent him from running in front of a moving car. Chuck's rants about petty government officials and sexually transmitted diseases continued all night long.

But when Chuck stripped naked in front of a local cathedral, police were called and he was taken to the Hospital of Hearts and Souls, where he appeared to be hallucinating. He was administered antipsychotic drugs.

The doctors told Chuck he had syphilis, a sexually transmitted disease that can move north in the body and cause havoc with the brain.

He was also told that he was an alcoholic. By 1959, this was probably evident to everyone in his life but him. Alcoholism in this era was hidden, kept in the closet—not unlike many other diseases like mental illness and cancer.

And once again, Ruth was tapped to rescue another male family member in distress in a far-flung place. She received a telegram: "Chuck hospitalized here with mental disorder. For his safety should fly home. Please wire immediately seven hundred dollars to Bank Indochina care Austrian consulate Papeete, covering fare and bills. Ted Johnson." ($700 is more than $7,500 in 2024 dollars.)

He protested his treatment in the Tahiti hospital in a letter to Ruth, describing some holes in the tops of his feet and in his hands, "as I was being crucified to my bed—and tied there for two days and two horrible nights."

Clearly, he explained to Ruth, the authorities and medical professionals did not understand his motives:

There was and still is a spiritual force within me that is more responsible than I—although I'm sure that those who watched me disrobe in front of the cathedral and walk naked to the door—I'm sure that not one of them realized or even thought for a moment, that I was compelled to do it. And that it was for a Purpose far greater than myself or those watching.

Over the next ten days, Chuck slept and dried out. And he became calmer and more lucid. In a "confession" in his journal, he expressed what turned out to be a rare appreciation for his mother:

*Forgiveness—Act of Contrition: Oh, Dear Mother Ruth, Mother of mine and daughter of Mary, and Jesus. You are a Saint. I tell you this, in order that you gain strength. Do not allow this to discouge [sic] your cause—but rather keep it to yourself and remember it only when you become lonely....
And while I write, the birds fly above, and guide me.*

When the medical professionals deemed him well enough to travel, and when Ruth's money arrived to pay his bills, he was discharged. As he packed his bags and headed to Quinn's for one farewell evening of drinking and guitar playing, he lamented about his life—and Joan Irvine: "I left Paul at the Vaihiria [lake] after telling him the story about Joan—how she is a saint, her sadness, and her money....I went directly to Quinn's. There was a group of three or four girls at the bar—and there was a man behind with a guitar. He was quite drunk—but he played beautifully and everyone was singing." Chuck sang cowboy songs for the crowd and was overcome with emotion. "I wanted to cry again. I knew I had to leave Tahiti and Quinn's. And so I walked outside."

10

THE GRIFTER

Services Offered: Furniture Refinishing & Renovating—An Assortment of Exhumations. The Lignum Vitae Company. Alan Graham, 420 Pomona Ave. 435-4620.
—*Advertisement placed by Alan Graham in the* Coronado Journal

E ven after he was paid for his work repairing Ruth Quinn's dining room table, local carpenter Alan Graham kept knocking on her door to "visit." Displeased with the quality of Alan's carpentry, Ruth was probably perplexed as to why this twenty-seven-year-old married man insisted on coming around to socialize with a seventy-one-year-old widow. Occasionally, he parked himself in a comfortable chair against the wall opposite the front door.

Facing him, mounted on a piece of gold velvet in a wooden shadow box, was a collection of antique cameos, a set of Italian pendants, bracelets and pins.

At least once, he commented on the vintage jewelry. Everyone did. They were unusual pieces. One was a double-headed cameo, and another featured two black-and-white Roman heads.

Ruth had inherited them from a beloved aunt. "She was an old lady when she died at the age of eighty-five in New York City in 1959. She was always very fond of me, and in her will she left me all of her personal possessions," Ruth testified in a 1972 deposition.

The cameos were part of her aunt's estate. "From the time I received them, I had the notion of enjoying them as display pieces rather than as jewels that I would be wearing. I am really not the cameo type. And so I had them mounted in a frame and they looked very beautiful."

Ruth never got them appraised. It never occurred to her to do so because she did not plan to sell them. And she was not raised to evaluate the economic value of a gift. It was only when they were stolen later that year, in October 1971, that she realized their worth. That's when it dawned on her: Alan Graham's visits had not been social calls. He was probably trying to figure out how to steal them from her.

She had met Alan on dressmaker Lelah Elgin's recommendation: "If you ever want to have any furniture refinished, this man is a very good workman." Ruth accepted Alan's business card. "An Assortment of Exhumations" was an interesting term to use to describe his business. Perhaps it was an allusion to his attempts to bury Ruth's jewels after he stole them. Ruth took Lelah's word and hired him on the spot.

Invited to inspect Ruth's broken dining room table, Alan showed up on Ruth's doorstep almost before she returned from Lelah's store. He inspected the table and carried it away to be repaired and refinished. He almost certainly took away a mental image of the case of antique cameos that he returned to steal.

Alan was a British expatriate who had been living on the island with his American wife for a few years, building a reputation as a skilled tradesman. He knew how to ingratiate himself with older, wealthy ladies who needed help around the house. He was charming and raffish, with an intriguing accent, droopy eyes and a shaggy head of hair. Born and raised in Liverpool, England, with thirteen brothers and sisters, Alan looked like he could have been a Beatle. In fact, he claimed he knew the foursome before they were famous.

It was 1971, and the bridge from the island to the mainland had been in operation for two years. Coronado had made more national

Alan Graham came to Coronado for the first time when he married Anne Morrison, sister to the Doors' front man Jim Morrison. *Quinn family.*

headlines that year, when President Richard Nixon hosted a state dinner for Mexican president Gustavo Díaz Ordaz at the Hotel del. More than one thousand people attended, including former president Lyndon Johnson and Lady Bird Johnson, Governor Ronald Reagan and Nancy Reagan, Frank Sinatra and John Wayne.

The Vietnam War was raging in Southeast Asia; many fathers and husbands from the island were fighting in it. A handful were also being held captive as prisoners-of-war (POWs) or were missing in action (MIAs). One of Ruth's neighbors, Sybil Stockdale, was the wife of one of the most senior POWs, Navy Commander Jim Stockdale. Sybil was leading a group of POW and MIA wives in an international campaign to raise awareness of the plight of their husbands—all from her living room at 547 A Avenue just a block from Ruth's home.

Alan was also a neighbor, who lived at 420 Pomona. On October 22, when Ruth was out with a group of lady friends at the opera, he and two accomplices broke into her home and stole the shadow box containing the cameos off the wall. Upon returning to 511 Pomona around 11:00 p.m., Ruth was greeted by her brother, Hank, who was sitting in her living room watching television—as he did many evenings. "When I walked in the house, I noticed my brother and not the cameos." Returning from the kitchen with a glass of wine and some cheese and crackers, "There was the empty wall. I had been in the house maybe five minutes."

She reported the theft to the Coronado Police Department the next afternoon. It was a mystery to her and everyone in Coronado who had stolen them and why, until one of Alan's accomplices was discovered more than two months later, on January 9, 1972—either early in the morning or late at night—digging in the sand near the seawall of rocks on Coronado's North Beach, ostensibly building a cache for the stolen goods.

Police arrested the accomplice, Coronado resident Charles Wilfred O'Hara, whose wife was a hair stylist at a local beauty salon. He took the police to his home, where the cameos were found. He probably implicated Alan, because Alan was arrested, along with two more accomplices: a twenty-two-year-old divorcée and rumored drug addict named Christine Yvonne Parsons Gies of 544 Glorietta Boulevard and a "transient" (as he was described in the newspaper—probably because he did not reside on the island) named William Brenner. The group had unsuccessfully tried to offload the stolen goods to a dealer in Los Angeles. The dealer declined to buy the cameos and reportedly tipped off the police. So it is likely that law enforcement was staking out Alan and his accomplices.

Alan Graham and his accomplices planned to bury here the cache of antique cameos they stole from Ruth Quinn. *Coronado Historical Association Collection.*

The case went to trial. Alan Graham was convicted of grand theft, conspiracy to commit theft and burglary. Gies and O'Hara were also convicted of receiving stolen property. Brenner was acquitted.

Gies received a sentence of one year in "honor camp," a type of prison work camp that operates on an honor system. O'Hara testified for the prosecution, so he received a modest $500 fine and three years of probation. Alan was handed the harshest sentence: 364 days in jail and three years of probation. If he had received just one more day of jail time, he could have been deported. His admiral father-in-law reportedly used his stature and influence to get Alan a lighter sentence.

On June 13, 1972, before his sentencing, Alan wrote Ruth an apology letter, of sorts. In it, he claimed his "innocence" but offered no contrition:

> *I can only ask that you in your wisdom, believe, that I would never knowingly cause you any unrest and certainly never take part in any plot to steal from you. I firmly believe that, in the future, I will be vindicated. Unfortunately, this affair extends beyond myself to affect my wife and family and her family and all the people who gave their trust to me.*

Indeed, the arrest, the conviction, the year in jail and the media coverage must have horrified Alan's wife. And it surely embarrassed her family, one that had already endured significant tragedy and embarrassment the year before from another family member: Jim Morrison. The front man for the legendary rock band the Doors was Alan's brother-in-law. He had been found dead in a bathtub in Paris in July 1971.

Jim had been estranged from his parents ever since he had avoided the draft and transformed himself from a clean-shaven short-haired Navy junior into the "Lizard King." The Morrison family learned of Jim's fame when the Doors' song "Light My Fire" reached #1 on the Billboard charts in 1967.

It was around this time that Alan married Jim Morrison's sister, Anne. They had met in London, where Anne was living with her parents, Navy Captain Steven Morrison and his wife, Clara. Captain Morrison, a career naval officer, was serving on the staff of the Commander in Chief U.S. Naval Forces Europe. Like Commander Charles Quinn, Captain Morrison was a Naval Academy graduate and naval aviator. Morrison flew combat missions in the Pacific theater of World War II and the Korean War.

And he played a role in the inauspicious beginning of the Vietnam War, what is known in the history books now as the Gulf of Tonkin incident.

From his flagship, the aircraft carrier USS *Bon Homme Richard*, Captain Morrison led the Seventh Fleet's Fifth Carrier Division in the Pacific, overseeing the local American forces.

On August 2, 1964, when North Vietnamese patrol boats strafed USS *Maddox*, one of the U.S. destroyers in his command that was patrolling off the coast of North Vietnam in the Tonkin Gulf, *Maddox* returned fire and damaged one of the North Vietnamese patrol boats. Claiming the attack was unprovoked, Captain Morrison put all his forces there on high alert.

But the attack on *Maddox* was provoked. It was retaliatory, in direct response to South Vietnamese commando attacks on North Vietnamese forces on the nearby island of Hòn Mê. Orchestrated behind the scenes by the United States, these island attacks were highly classified. Few in the U.S. military chain of command knew that the United States was assisting the South Vietnamese forces in these raids on Hòn Mê.

Two days later, on August 4, based on reports of a *second* incoming and unprovoked attack, Morrison authorized even more aggressive counterattacks by two ships, *Maddox* and destroyer USS *Turner Joy.*

Portrait photo of Rear Admiral G.S. Morrison, USN, taken by PH1 T.L. Williams, June 21, 1967. *U.S. Navy.*

No evidence of a second attack was discovered—no North Vietnamese patrol boats, no wreckage, no casualties in the water. Morrison and his division had been spooked.

Convincing the American people that U.S. forces were the victims of two unprovoked attacks, President Lyndon Johnson ordered retaliatory strikes on North Vietnam on August 5, 1964, and sought Congressional authority to wage war under the Gulf of Tonkin Resolution, passed by Congress and signed on August 10.

This series of events provided President Lyndon Johnson the justification he needed to start the Vietnam War. Captain Steve Morrison's son Jim had avoided that war—escaping imminent draft by running away. He soon became a leading cultural symbol of everyone who was against the Vietnam War.

Over the next seven years, Jim Morrison's lyrics, some written in Coronado, became anthems railing against everything his father's generation stood for and defended.

Captain Morrison was promoted to rear admiral at the age of forty-seven. He reached the top ranks of the Navy just as his son was topping the music charts. But the great generational divide between the two of them was too deep a chasm to cross. Jim told reporters his parents were dead. For many years, Rear Admiral and Mrs. Morrison refused to speak publicly about him.

In London with her parents, Anne Morrison was attending college when she met Alan. He said he was born and raised poor in dirty postwar Liverpool. His father was, as he called him, a "rag man." Some said his father was a con man.

Anne and Alan married and conceived their first child in London. Rear Admiral Morrison was ordered to Washington, D.C., for a short stint before being sent back to the Pacific Fleet. The Morrison family took up residence in Coronado in a house at 135 H Avenue. Alan and Anne followed.

Alan was introduced to the Coronado naval community, as well as its dark underbelly. Alan had spent time in reform school in England, punishment for stealing. So he already had a record as a thief. In Coronado, he began his career as a grifter. He was a skilled carpenter, so it was not surprising that he sought work from the island locals. But he also made acquaintances with some of its shadier characters. One was Ed "Bud" Bernhard, a World War II B-17 tail gunner who later became a talented bricklayer. Bernhard also ran an illegal abortion mill on the island.

Alan was also probably familiar with the teenagers in town who were running a marijuana drug trade across the border between Mexico and Coronado. They swam from the beaches of Tijuana to Imperial Beach, towing the product behind them, smuggling right under the noses of Coronado parents and local officials. When the kids started throwing around one-hundred-dollar bills in bars and restaurants and driving shiny new cars around the island, eyebrows were raised.

This criminal band of water polo players and Coronado lifeguards recruited their high school Spanish teacher to serve as the group's translator and ringleader. Over the next ten years, what was dubbed the Coronado Company built their business into a $100 million global operation. It was the largest on the West Coast, importing ninety million tons of product from all over the world.

It was not until 1981 that they were caught after an exhaustive multiyear investigation by the Drug Enforcement Administration. More than one hundred people were indicted, and many spent time in prison.

Why did Alan Graham and his accomplices steal the cameos? Perhaps they were in search of fast cash—just like the Coronado Company kids were enjoying. And why did they plan to bury them in the sand on Coronado Beach?

Before he was released from prison in 1973, Alan published a pamphlet of poetry that he titled *Poet Rain*. He mailed a copy to Ruth. In it, he crafted an ode to his dead brother-in-law:

"In Loving Memory of James Douglas Morrison R.I.P."
By Alan R. Graham

The music dragon got him
Down in Texas that night.
It stole his soul
And made him cry.

After this early swivel
The bright midnight came
And haunting green scores
From an obedient violin.

All of his ladies
Who are snake charmers
And sidewalk opera singers,
Sent silent flowers over
Parisian telephone poles of white.

He is sleeping slowly
In Pere Lachaise
With all the other word wizards
Before him.

Sometimes in wettest nights
Strangers arrive to see his name
Carved between the ivy
And the rain.

It was the first of many songs, poems and books Alan would write about his famous brother-in-law over the course of his life. Back in Coronado after his prison stint, he and his wife, Anne, continued to grow their family, and he continued working as a carpenter. But he also began to capitalize on his familial relationship with Jim Morrison, whose fame was climbing after his 1971 death. The singer achieved cult status in the 1970s. His legacy over the next five decades and sales of his music skyrocketed. Alan would spend the rest of his life trying to cash in.

11
BILLS AND BREAKDOWNS

I have been very depressed, very tired, and very discouraged—partly over the facts of my life, but mostly over my failures, with regard to those facts....I cannot accept any credit for prayers for Chuck's sad affairs. I am grateful that it seems to be clearing up. I hope the little girl will be happy. Always....Heaven only knows when I will see you again.
—Letter from Ruth Quinn to Mother Clarke, March 4, 1975

Ruth did not get out much in the winter of 1975. Her brother, Hank, was keeping her cooped up. He had moved into her home after his latest skin cancer surgery on his face and required her to be his nurse for a few weeks. Ever the caretaker.

In the last letter she wrote to her son, Ruth—who held Chuck's purse strings—was complaining about Hank while also wringing her hands over her fixed income and her increasing need to rely on her monthly widow's benefits to make ends meet. "Isn't it strange how many times the first of the month falls on a weekend?" Was it an attempt at levity? Or was she stalling, resisting her son's demands for cash?

Indeed, all Ruth's letters to Chuck included subtle reminders of her challenges in funding Chuck's lifestyle—something he was unable to do for himself.

In early 1975, Chuck Quinn was almost forty-two years old. Unlike many of his childhood friends from Coronado who were pursuing careers in the Navy, in education, in medicine and in law, his career had not taken off. The buddies he had caroused with in Tijuana, Oahu, Windansea, Alta, Tahoe and Tahiti were achieving professional success and building families. Chuck was stuck. He had never seemed to fully recover from his mental breakdown in Tahiti in 1959.

Upon being discharged from the hospital in Tahiti that year, Chuck flew home. At the San Diego airport, Ruth met him with a pair of strong hospital aides and a straitjacket. He was taken against his wishes to a local sanatorium, where he was given shock treatments on his mother's orders.

Shock treatments: the colloquial term for electroconvulsive therapy, or ECT. This "therapy," first introduced in the 1950s, uses electric shocks to the brain to induce seizures. Some thought the treatment mitigated symptoms of mental illness, like depression and schizophrenia. Some called it medical abuse.

And the early treatment practices seemed barbaric: patients were awake and held down by nurses, while a bit was placed in their mouths and electrodes were placed on their temples. Then electric shocks were administered for several seconds. It was painful and exhausting. It did cause memory loss, sometimes long-term. Some patients experienced mania and paranoia after treatments.

According to John Elwell, these treatments left Chuck a "complete vegetable," unable to function for days. And the recovery was slow. The trauma he endured from this experience bred deep resentment toward his mother. Despite those feelings, he never became financially independent from her.

After his treatment ended, he decided to head to Alta, Utah, for another winter of skiing, leaving his medical bills behind for Ruth to settle: "January 13, 1960—Alta, Utah—…I hate to mention this again to you, but it is rather important. I still have not received a completed claim statement from Dr. Kiser. Please call his office for me. Also, how about the statement from Central Drug?…P.S. Just a reminder—you should have received a notice of premium due for one of the insurance policies—due 9/5/59. Has it been paid yet?"

This request became a pattern.

Ruth started sending Chuck a monthly allowance of $300 (more than $1,700 in 2024 dollars). It was never enough. He repeatedly asked her for help with his rent, his medical and dental bills, his car repairs and even his vacations. Although he pursued many jobs and professions, he could not keep steady work or earn a reliable income.

Over the next fifteen years, Chuck pursued medical school, sales positions, construction jobs, photography and writing assignments and consulting gigs.

Nothing panned out. He was always broke and hitting up Ruth for money. Ruth acquiesced, sending him more and more.

His sense of entitlement seemed to clash wildly with his deep sense of shame in asking her for money, repeatedly. Their relationship vacillated between loving words and hateful words. Every visit ended in shouting matches and accusations, followed by apology letters—and more requests for money.

It was a battle of words, wills and wealth:

December 10, 1960
Dear Mom,
Thank you so much for your letter and the money order. Things were getting a little low—and it hit me just right. I will pay you back when I get home as I should get about $125 for my car.

In 1964, Chuck decided he wanted to try to go to medical school. He moved to Utah to take premed classes:

Saturday, 9-22-64—Jackson, Wyoming

I'm registered now and school starts at 8:50 Monday morning. I'm now a Zoology major, and a candidate for a degree in June....In the meantime, I will be completing my applications to medical school....P.S. I thoroughly enjoyed your last most thoughtful letter. Thank you. Also, just a reminder to send my check as soon as you can because there have been lots of expenses.

In 1965, Chuck was facing a whole lot more expenses, of the legal kind. Chuck and Ruth were slapped with a paternity lawsuit from an ex-fiancée, the mother of Chuck's first child:

July 5, 1965
My dearest Chuck,
Now that I have every reason to believe that you know that I know I feel free to write! I wanted to wait until I heard from you—but I can understand your not writing.
Of course I am very worried about you. Ever since I received that shattering telephone call on June 21st from Ann's lawyer, followed a few days later by a long letter from Ann. You have been on my mind day and night.

This is hardly the time for reproach or recrimination. I feel too guilty myself, because I know that I must have failed you miserably over the years or this situation would never have arisen. For two weeks my whole being has been rocked with every possible emotion but I am calm now—and my only concern is you.

If I am suffering, I can only imagine how you are suffering—but it's done now and the only thing to do now is to put your trust in God that "all will be well.". . .

Only Mother Clarke and Lowell Davies know the story—I had to talk to someone and I needed to legally because of Mr. H's threats. Uncle Hank knows nothing and as far as I am concerned never will!!

Now let me make a few suggestions:

1ˢᵗ—Tell the whole story to Dr. Popper—better that you tell him—than Mr. H—and he will tell him if he hasn't already done so!

2ⁿᵈ—Change your residence back to California as soon as you can and also your automobile place and license

3ʳᵈ—Get a good lawyer in San Francisco—if possible a Catholic

And last talk things over with a good friend like Mr. Nideman [sic]. You have always tried to go it alone. It's better to share your problems and sorrows. I keep thinking of that waterfront man you told me about. Talk to him.

"This too shall pass," my dear son—not too easily, but time takes care of most things.

I am not going to preach. All I ask is that you take care of your health— and keep up your spirits.

What you did was not uncommon in this day and age—and Ann is just as culpable—maybe more so.

I am not going to say anything more now. Let me hear from you. Mothers have a way of understanding, forgiving, and continuing to love their children.

There are many solutions to the problem—but it is for you to choose what is best for all concerned. If you want me at any time, I am standing by.

God bless and keep you—so much love,
Mother

By 1966, plans for medical school had been abandoned. Abandoned, too, was the baby he fathered in Utah in 1965. He took Ruth's advice and moved back to San Francisco, where he continued to search for a career and a salary. Meanwhile, he relied on Ruth for supplements.

Ruth was still in the caregiving business for Hank, who was as demanding as Chuck:

> *January 29, 1966*
> *My dearest Chuck,*
> *It was wonderful to talk to you last Saturday. Too bad you overheard the bickering, but you are unwise to let it disturb you. I appreciate your concern, but don't let this worry you. Look at it this way. As long as I resist Hank, I am still in the driver's seat. Once I give in, as grandmother finally did, I have cooked my own goose. That can delay your own progress, and if that includes me, it's alright with me.... Will you let me know soon whether you want me to pay your rent—and loan, as I did, at your request, last month?...Hank is not well, true enough, but he is also very spoilt, very demanding and uses his nervousness to get his own way. Don't let all this disturb you. You are no longer a part of it. This is my problem and I am very hopeful that it will be solved in the not too distant future. The one thing necessary for you is to put aside anything and everything family.*

At one point, Chuck characterized Ruth's handouts as "loans," though he never seemed to repay them:

> *March 14, 1968*
> *Dear Mother,*
> *Thank you for sending me the loan. I will attempt to repay you in one year. In the meantime, I am inclosing [sic] a promissory note with this letter.*

Chuck seemed to have no shame in his requests:

> *25 June 1969*
> *Dear Mother,*
> *When I last spoke with you on the telephone, you said you would send me $500.00 for this coming month also. I hope you can do it. In fact I had the misfortune to loose [sic] my sunglasses which cost me $65.00 to replace, so if you could possibly send more than $500 I would greatly appreciate it.*

Sometimes the pleas for financial assistance were polite:

April 1, 1970
I read how people on fixed incomes are hurting economically more and more and I realize from what you say in your letters that it is a great personal sacrifice for you to keep sending me $300 each month. Nevertheless, I ask again, with hopes and prayers that soon I will find regular employment. Thank you for all your help.
Love,
Chuck

And sometimes they were not:

August 5, 1971
Dear Mother,
Your note, and your check for $440.00 just arrived. Thank you. Let me take this opportunity to remind you:
(1) I have not asked you for an additional monthly allowance of $140—or $100—or any other amount. I did write to you with a request for $100 additional, this month only, for medical bills.
(2) You may also recall, that in Jan., Feb., Mar., Apr., and May of this year you sent me a monthly allowance of $350. That was $50 more each month than during the previous year. I did not ask for it. You volunteered it, saying that the increased cost of living warranted it, and that you had sold your Heide stock, etc. I welcomed the additional $50 per month—as well as the $500 bonus I received on January 22, 1971 and the $50.00 on March 25th while I was in San Diego for Dr. Pickering.
(3) In June and July 1971 my monthly allowance was reduced by you to $300.00—without any explanation or warning.
I do not intend to participate further in any game situation with you in regards to money—or anything else. I think it is about time that you begin to live and act like a mature person. You agreed to send me a monthly allowance. I expect to receive it on time, i.e., during the first four days of each month.
If you are having troubles in your life, I suggest you communicate with someone of competence for help in those matters.

And of course, money for vacation would be nice:

Sept. 12, 1972
Dear Mother,
Thank you for your Labor Day letter and my monthly allowance....I'm getting ready myself, this week, to leave on Sunday for a back-pack into the Wind River Mountains of Wyoming....I usually wander for about two weeks. This will be my 4th fall in the Rockies so I'm beginning to feel quite at home in the Wilderness....Would you please send my October check air mail to me in Pinedale, Wyo. so that I can take care of my rent by mail from there?

And when the monthly allowance was not enough, another plea for a "loan" arrived:

January 7, 1973
Dear Mother,
This is a plea for help, i.e., if there is any available. With the lack of work and the diminished unemployment insurance available for me, I have gotten a little behind in paying some outstanding accounts payable....I wish to borrow as much as you can afford to loan me at this time. I think I can pay you back within three months.

Of course, appealing to Ruth's sense of piety probably played well:

March 14, 1973
Mother Clarke's influence in our lives has been remarkable. Her long ambition of reconciling us is succeeding. I think that we accept one another now, in all our weaknesses—as we have never done before. Please pray with me that I will become financially independent.

After what turned out to be Chuck's final visit with his mother, over the holidays of 1974, he sent one of his last communiqués to her. It seemed like a heartfelt note of appreciation:

December 30, 1974
Dear Mother,
It was a swell Christmas for me—a really beautiful day. Thank you for coming to the airport to meet me. I enjoyed our walk and Mass together. It was nice that Uncle Hank joined us in church and that our old friend, Monsignor Purcell, offered the Mass.

It was a wonderful dinner that you prepared and served so well. Thanks for all your work & effort.

Thank you, too, for your generous Christmas check. I'll use that money to go skiing—probably soon to Carson City—with the Flynn family.

Keep well, and happy in 1975. Thanks again for making my Christmas so joyous. I'll be going soon to see Mother Clarke and I will deliver your candy to her. I'm enclosing a thank you note to Mrs. Mulcahy. Will you mail it to her for me?

Love, Chuck

Money and a lack of work were not Chuck's only worries. While battling the paternity lawsuit from the woman in Utah, Chuck was involuntarily hospitalized again.

And after a late-night bender in Tijuana, he crashed his car and almost killed himself on the highway returning to Coronado. His car was totaled, and his surgeon told him he might not walk again.

He was lucky: the surgeon performed "magic," according to Chuck, repairing the bone and successfully transplanting tendons.

He called it his "holy accident." Chuck recovered physically and recognized his addiction. "I was a lonely, isolated alcoholic, estranged from society, never having been a part of it. I was addicted to alcohol. Then I found a new way of living. I got sober."

And he *did* get sober that year, attending AA on a regular basis for decades. He remained sober for the rest of his life.

Living in a small studio apartment in San Francisco, near the Embarcadero, he spent his days organizing his papers, walking around the city, hiking in Marin County on Mount Tamalpais and attending Mass. Whether or not it was his intention, he was becoming a loner.

Chuck lamented that he could not seem to fit in anywhere—except on the slopes and the waves, where he had no responsibilities. Skimming the mountain powder and the ocean foam, soaring like a bird, above the fray—this was where he excelled and could prove himself. There, he felt like a man and at peace with the universe.

Peace was shattered by the reality of his actions. In February 1975, the paternity lawsuit that the mother of his first child filed in 1965 was finally settled, releasing him from all "past, present, and future obligations in regards to her daughter and bringing about the dismissal of all constraints in the state of Utah."

A street photographer captured Ruth and Chuck walking down Powell Street in San Francisco in 1964. *Esky Kurtz.*

Obviously feeling relieved of any parental responsibility for a child in Utah, he must have been shocked to find out that just as he was settling this lawsuit, another girlfriend, in San Francisco, was pregnant and due to deliver a baby in August 1975. He was going to be a father again.

Chuck dismissed his girlfriend, telling her: "I just can't handle this right now."

This latest wrinkle could only have added to his level of stress. Boxed in, needing to exhale and still without solid employment, Chuck decided that month that he was going to take a trip to Carson City to hike and ski in nearby Lake Tahoe and to visit his old Coronado friend Dr. Pat Flynn and his family.

He also really wanted to join pal John Elwell in Ireland that summer, where John was going to be attending graduate school. A week before Ruth was murdered, Chuck told John that he was going to ask Ruth, once again, for vacation money.

12

A CALL TO DR. EATON

The shoes have always bothered me.
—*Victor Caloca, former San Diego cold case detective, in 2006*

R uth," Hank called out as he entered 511 Pomona Avenue, or so he told the Coronado Police. It was around 10:15 p.m. on Sunday, March 16, 1975. As was his habit, Hank had arrived to spend the night in Ruth's second bedroom. The porch light she had installed after the cameo theft in 1971 was switched off. The kitchen and bedroom lights were on and so was the television.

Ruth did not answer Hank. He told police he walked to the back bedroom, where he spied her lying on her bed, her legs partially covered with a bedspread. She was wearing her church clothes and jewelry, as well as nylons and her black high-heeled shoes. A pillow with bullet holes and powder burns lay next to her. The left side of her face and her left hand were smudged with blood. A pool of blood was coagulating on the sheets under her head. There were two gunshot wound entry points: one on the right side of her neck and one behind her right ear.

"I shook her and called out her name," Hank said. She was probably already cold to the touch.

He said he was confused.

So what did he do? He picked up the phone and called the family doctor, Charles Eaton (no relation to Eatons' Ranch). Dr. Eaton was a beloved and trusted family physician to several generations of Coronado residents, the type who still made house calls. And while a dial to 911 might have seemed more logical today, doctors during this era were sometimes the first person a family turned to in times of distress. Dr. Eaton, a World War II and Korean War Navy veteran, was the first man to perform surgical operations on a beachhead, in Korea. He earned two Bronze Stars during that war. But his Navy career was cut short when he contracted polio four weeks after returning home from the war, paralyzing him from the waist down. Nonetheless, he continued seeing seven to eight hundred patients a month from a wheelchair, until he was medically retired in 1953. With intense physiotherapy, Dr. Eaton recovered his ability to walk unassisted, although he used canes to get up and down stairs. Given Dr. Eaton's disability, he could not have arrived very quickly.

While he waited for Dr. Eaton, Hank said, he knocked on the door of Ruth's neighbor, Cynthia Parker Callahan. There was no response.

Dr. Eaton and his wife, Jeannette, arrived, and Hank met them outside the house. Entering 511 Pomona Avenue, Dr. Eaton examined Ruth and immediately called the Coronado Police Department.

Dr. Charles Eaton, personal physician to Ruth Quinn and Hank Leyendecker and the first person Hank called when he discovered Ruth's body. Also pictured is Dr. Eaton's second wife, Jane. *Caroline Murray.*

At some point, Hank also called Monsignor John Purcell, the Irish-born priest at Sacred Heart who had known Hank and Ruth for more than thirty years. Hank also called Laura Christian. Both Monsignor Purcell and Laura rushed over.

The Coronado Police Department sent Officer Don Erbe and Sergeant Dick Solomon, who arrived at 10:32 p.m.—seventeen minutes after Hank said he entered the house. By that time, a crowd had assembled: Hank, Laura, Dr. and Mrs. Eaton and Monsignor Purcell—all wandering around the crime scene.

Hank and Dr. Eaton greeted the policemen at the door. Dr. Eaton explained why he was at the scene. "Ruth is my patient," Dr. Eaton told them. "She was in good general health, her only illness being high blood pressure."

Officers Erbe and Solomon most likely called Coronado police chief Art LeBlanc, who arrived a few minutes later. As the police officers looked around, they noted there was no sign of forced entry and that it appeared Ruth had been in the process of cooking dinner around the time she was killed. On the kitchen counter was an open cookbook, a cucumber, some tomatoes and a partially peeled onion. On the oven was a neatly stacked row of spices and a pot filled with a white soup substance. The oven was on, and inside was a pot of rice, dried and shriveled.

Everything in Ruth's kitchen and bedroom was neat and tidy, except for her jewelry box, where two drawers were found open. A book of psalms lay on her bedroom desk, along with photos of Chuck and Michael as young boys and religious icons. Lots of religious icons.

Chief LeBlanc, portly and balding, began shuffling through papers and books on the desk. He picked up the telephone in Ruth's bedroom to make a few calls.

One of the calls LeBlanc made was to Coronado police detective Paul Dodson, who arrived just as everyone else was leaving. "You got it!" LeBlanc told him. The case was his. Dodson was left alone with the body until the coroner arrived.

Young and trim with chiseled features, a Roman nose and sideburns, Dodson had grown up in Coronado, having moved there in 1954. Like his stepdad, he joined the Navy right after graduating from Coronado High School. But, "Ever since I was safety patrol in the sixth grade, I knew I wanted to work in law enforcement." Now, with nine years of experience on the force in Coronado, he had his biggest case yet. His first interview was going to be with Hank, his second with Alan Graham.

And where was Chuck? In Carson City, Nevada, 535 miles and a nine-hour drive from Coronado.

Police called the home of Dr. Pat Flynn, where Chuck had been a houseguest since March 12. He had driven from San Francisco in his distinctive green Mustang, one he kept in mint condition and locked up with a bolt and chain.

Answering the phone late that Sunday night, Pat told the Coronado police that Chuck was indeed their houseguest, but he had been gone all day hiking or skiing with friends—he had not been with the Flynns. Pat promised to have Chuck call the police as soon as he returned.

Pat and Chuck had attended Coronado High School together and remained friends, even through Chuck's periods of erratic behavior, when other childhood friends had cut ties with him. When Chuck visited the Flynns, he slept in the bedroom of the Flynns' older daughter (who was away at college) or in the camper parked in their driveway. Sometimes he took the Flynns' eighteen-year-old son, Patrick, hiking or camping.

It is not clear when Chuck returned to the Flynns' house, but the next morning, Monday, March 17, at approximately 11:30 a.m., Pat sat Chuck down and soberly shared the news: his mother was dead, murdered. "I remember how distressed he was to receive the news," Pat's younger daughter, Monica, recalled. She was sixteen years old at the time. Dr. Flynn's son Patrick agreed: "He was very distraught."

Chuck immediately called the Coronado Police Department, and they confirmed that his mother had been killed sometime between 4:00 p.m. and 10:00 p.m. the day before. Her body was at the San Diego Coroners' Office.

Coronado police chief Art LeBlanc in the Coronado Fourth of July parade, circa 1970s. *Joe Ditler.*

Two detectives from San Diego were being brought in to work on the case: George Crawford and a rookie named Jack Drown, a man who would later become the police chief for Coronado.

Chuck got in his car and headed home to San Francisco, alone with his thoughts for the four-hour drive. What were his last words to his mother?

With him was a church program from St. Teresa of Avila Catholic Church in Carson City for a service on March 16, 1975, the day his mother was shot to death. Did he save the leaflet for posterity, to mark the day his mother died, or as an alibi? He kept everything from that week— receipts, diary entries and detailed date-stamped notes of every phone call, meeting and conversation he had in the weeks following his mother's murder. Almost five decades later, every single one of these files was still neatly organized in his apartment.

The next day, Tuesday, March 18, Chuck flew to Coronado. He had to plan his mother's funeral. Amid the many questions probably flooding his mind was a pressing one he needed answering before his April rent was due: Was he her heir?

13

TWO ROOSTERS AND A HEN

Coronado Slaying Remains Puzzle
—San Diego Union *headline, March 18, 1975*

T wo days after his mother's death, Chuck drove south to the scene of the crime. At the apex of the bridge onto Coronado was a familiar sight: the entire expanse of the island laid out in front of him. To the left was the city golf course, where a clutch of players was scattered, even on a weekday. A row of houses lined the course, several of which backed onto his mother's cottage. Had any of the neighbors seen or heard anything on Sunday night?

As he descended from the bridge onto Third Street, signs of spring were everywhere. The birds were boisterous, and the flowers were popping. Easterners do not believe that California has a noticeable spring, but they are wrong. Beginning in March, Coronado bursts with the emergence of roses, birds of paradise, bougainvillea, oranges, lavender, rosemary and the acrid fragrance of eucalyptus trees that line the roads. In preparation for the city's annual flower show that takes place the first weekend of April, Coronado's residents were pruning and primping their gardens and flower boxes for the judges who toured every front yard and gave out first-, second- and third-place awards. Residents take pride in earning these ribbons and hang them in their windows.

Chuck had to approach Ruth's cottage slowly.

The home and Ruth's 1969 Chevy Impala in the carport were walled off by police tape, the door padlocked, with a hot pink police sticker pasted over it, forbidding entry. Chuck could not access her car or any of the contents of her house. When was he going to be able to get in? He wanted a police escort. And what about the crime scene? Was he going to have to clean it up?

He left and checked into the Crown City Motor Inn. From there, he began his meticulous preparations for the funeral Mass—without any apparent help from his uncle. "The funeral [home] director asked if I wanted to see the body." Having attended medical school for a short period of time, he probably was not squeamish at the sight of dead bodies. Years later, he recounted, without emotion, "There were two shots behind the ear."

He arranged for a crucifix, a rosary and an Apostleship of Prayers to be blessed and placed in her casket. He ordered flowers and ribbons to adorn it. The Heide family in New York and New Jersey also sent flowers for the altar. Chuck asked local friends and parishioners Bill Adams, Bud Bernhard, Joe McDonough, Frank Jennings, Bob Capitanich, Rear Admiral Joe Callahan, Pat Callahan, Jim Brill, George McGuire and Bill VanVleck to serve as pallbearers.

Not Hank. He was assigned no role in the funeral or the burial.

Chuck resented Hank, a guy who lived off his mother, Chuck's grandmother, until she died and then depended on his sister Ruth for the rest of his life. "It was sad and dangerous," Chuck believed, like Hank was a prisoner of sorts. He claimed that Hank was caught in what he called the "money-inheritance trap," an affliction he believed Hank suffered his whole life.

It was an affliction from which Chuck too, suffered but did not acknowledge.

Hank thought Chuck was "a mooch and a phony." And Hank might have known about the paternity lawsuit, given how much time he spent with Ruth. He also might have been more than a little concerned about Chuck squandering an inheritance from Ruth. Indeed, a few weeks before Ruth's murder, she paid a visit to a fellow librarian on the island. This trusted friend was married to a minister, so Ruth felt doubly sure she could count on the couple's confidence and pastoral advice. Their daughter was present for the kitchen table talk, where Ruth seemed agitated. She confided to them: her brother wanted her to turn over control of her securities—the inheritance she received from her mother—to him. She was apparently quite distressed about the pressure from him.

When Ruth turned up dead, the librarian and her husband were so disturbed over the murder and what Ruth had shared with them in confidence that they filled in their back doorway with concrete, covered up their windows with bars and bolted out of town for a few weeks. The minister considered taking a job with another parish in another state.

What scared them so much? What did Ruth say about Hank and his badgering? Why did they feel threatened by her murder? Were they afraid of Hank?

And why did he want to take control of her inheritance? Hank did not need the money. He had his *own* inheritance from their mother. Did he want to prevent Chuck from getting any of it? Had he come to resent what a pushover Ruth had become with Chuck? The tensions between Hank and Ruth seemed as taut as they were between Chuck and Ruth.

Hank and Chuck were more alike than either one would admit. They were two roosters—erudite, haughty playboys who let everyone know of their heritage as descendants of Henry Heide. They were thrifty. Both were athletic. And each was resentful of a lifetime of domineering henpecking from Ruth.

"It created a tremendous amount of tension between us," Chuck admitted. All three of them.

Was it possible Chuck knew that Hank was pressuring Ruth for control of her securities? Did that contribute to his urgency to find the will? Chuck was aggressive in his inquiries and requests to become the executor of her estate. The day he got to Coronado, only two days after his mother's death, Chuck tried to meet with Ruth's prominent San Diego lawyer, Lowell Davies, the same Lowell Davies who had handled his paternity lawsuit. Chuck needed his mother's will and the requisite paperwork to make him the estate's executor. And he wanted it quickly.

Chuck claimed for many years after the murder that he was unsure whether he was the beneficiary of Ruth's estate: "It turned out that my mother left everything that she owned to me. I didn't know that until after her death. You know she never told me."

But Chuck *did* know. In a letter to her in 1965, he made it clear that he would prefer to have his inheritance before she died:

> *Dear Mother,*
> *Thank you for your recent letter and for sending the check.... This business of you and Hank always saying to me—"It will all be yours when we are gone—you will be sitting pretty"—is a lot of hogwash. Let's face facts and be honest with ourselves for once: In ten years, I'll be making all the money that I'll ever need—I am not an extravagant person and never have been.*

My tastes are for the best—but I seldom buy and what's more I take care of what I do buy. It lasts.

If I decided now to make money, it would be simple—What I want to do requires that I get out and work with people—people who can't afford to pay me in cash but pay me great dividends in understanding, knowledge, and satisfaction. I never have and never will be impressed with money—I don't care a damn about it—except for certain conveniences. I am a "socialist" at heart and I am going to devote my life to seeing that social justice—i.e., the inhuman use of the poor by the rich is eliminated from the environment. So don't go into the old family routine of wealth etc.—and inheritance etc.— If you want to really do something for me come thru now when the need is there—not a week or a year latter [sic] when it is too damn late anyway. Best of luck,

Chuck

14
PIROUETTES

Prayerful Remembrance Requested: Mrs. Ruth Quinn Dies: The parish and community were saddened by the violent death of a beloved citizen of our city. Services are scheduled for Monday and Tuesday of this week. Rosary will be recited in the Church on Monday evening at 7:30, and Mass will be celebrated on Tuesday morning at 10. Burial will follow at Fort Rosecrans Cemetery. May she rest in peace!
—Sacred Heart Catholic Church program, Sunday, March 23, 1975

The night before Ruth's funeral, police guarded her body at Sacred Heart. When the islanders began arriving for the Mass in her honor the next day, the police were watching.

All the regular parishioners showed up, as did most of the old-timers from the island who knew and liked Ruth: friends from the library; fellow fans of the San Diego Opera, where she was a regular patron; Pink Ladies from the Coronado Hospital, where she volunteered; fellow members of the Society of Military Widows; teachers from Coronado High School, where she taught opera classes; members of the Coronado Women's Club; and many nuns from the College of Women in San Diego—where she had spent so many hours setting up and organizing the library.

After the assembly had filled the pews, Hank entered the church. He walked down the nave and stopped next to the front pew. As if on stage, he outstretched his arms and performed an exaggerated pirouette, a silent dance with an imaginary partner. He told his regular tennis buddies that he and Ruth used to dance together as children to open society season events in Manhattan. This performance was his final tribute to her.

It was probably best that Chuck did not witness Hank's display of affectation. The tension between them had reached a boiling point. When Chuck filed in and found Hank sitting next to the casket, he revolted. "As the son, I felt *I* had preference, you know? We were in the same pew, side by side, just the two of us." Chuck did his own little pirouette, whipping around and ordering the ushers: "Please remove him."

After the Mass, the mourners proceeded to Fort Rosecrans, a veterans cemetery perched on both sides of the hilltop peninsula of Point Loma. Even with the morning marine layer of fog hanging over the city, there was a clear vista of all of San Diego Bay, the entire island of Coronado and the airstrips of North Island and even Tijuana in the distance. There, with a brisk ocean breeze blowing, Ruth's casket, covered with a spray of white daisies, was lowered into a grave next to her husband's and a few feet away from the grave of little Michael.

Chuck described the scene in a letter to his old friend John Elwell:

> *At my mother's graveside two weeks ago, on Tuesday, March 25, up on Pt. Loma at Fort Rosecrans next to the grave of my father and a few yards down and across the hill from my brother Michael's grave, I looked down through the mist and rain while the cold wind blew, and saw the jetty at North Island. I could see precisely where we put the lobster trap many years ago. And I traced our path back along the beach from where we carried it from the Life Guard Station in the sand below the Officers' Club. Beyond was North Beach, Center Beach, the Hotel, the Strand swinging in a long curve to the Sloughs, and Mexico below. The Coronado Islands seemed close and the ocean was flat where we raced Evening Star.*
>
> *It is all past. A new life begins. I accepted my mother. I loved her as best I could, realizing her limitations and inability to love me. She did the best she could. She tried very hard. We worked on it together, under the guidance of our spiritual counselor Mother Genevieve Clarke, R.S.C.J., who is 93 now and living not far from here at Menlo Park. We had made tremendous strides towards reconciliation. There was always the interference of my mother's relationship with her brother, which dominated each of their lives, and directly effected [sic] the death of my brother and father, and which undoubtedly began when the two of them were children.*
>
> *Whoever murdered my mother robbed each of us of the opportunity to have completely reconciled, and so I feel cheated. But we almost made it. Certainly we came a long long way.*

112

She was an interesting and complex woman. Deeply spiritual. Close to God, in agony and pain. Poorly adapted to life. Everything was a struggle for her. Nothing was easy. Not her death either.

It has been hard…

Gunker

Clockwise from top left: The headstones of Ruth Quinn; her husband, Commander Charles Quinn; and her younger son, Michael Joseph Quinn, at Rosecrans National Veterans Cemetery, Point Loma, California. *Author's collection*; The grave of Mother Genevieve Clarke at the Sacred Heart Convent Cemetery in Menlo Park, California. She was Ruth's coworker, friend, confidante and spiritual advisor and died just a few months after Ruth's murder. *Lee Dorsey.*

15

THREATS AND RUMORS

Jesus, Mary and Joseph, I give you my heart and soul; Jesus, Mary and Joseph, assist me in my last agony; Jesus, Mary and Joseph, let me breathe forth my spirit in peace with you.
—Prayers for a Happy Death, *a handwritten poem left on Ruth's doorstep*

Ruth had confided to one of her friends, Coronado civic activist Mary Carlin King, that she had "premonitions" of being murdered.

Apparently, the forebodings were aroused by threatening phone calls. The phone started ringing soon after the 1972 cameo theft trial, the one that put Alan Graham behind bars. The caller was allegedly the mother of Christie Gies, Alan's female accomplice in the theft of the antique jewels. Gies was rumored to be a drug addict, one of the island alley cats with whom Alan cavorted. The caller threatened to "make things worse" for Ruth.

Gies and her mother lived on the same block as Ruth, behind her house, facing the golf course, at 544 Glorietta Boulevard—a stone's throw away from her cottage. Too close for comfort.

The calls rattled Ruth. Her home address had been listed in newspaper accounts of the burglary for anyone to read. And her phone number was published in the Coronado phone book. The district attorney advised Ruth to change her phone number to an unlisted one, which she did.

According to friends and locals, Ruth was threatened in other ways, as well.

Her Coronado Women's Club friends claimed she had confided in them, at different times, that she had received letters threatening her life.

Chuck's longtime friend from the island Esky Kurtz told him a haunting rumor: "Aunt Jane Reynolds [the mother of Kingston Trio singer Nick Reynolds, a Coronado classmate of Chuck's] told me that one of her sisters was among a group of women who lunched with your mother on the day she was killed. When she rose to leave, your mother said, 'Goodbye, girls, I'll see you tomorrow if I don't get shot first.'"

In the weeks immediately following Ruth's death, the "dirt"—the whodunit postmortems—started piling up around town. The rumor mill was churning. Who would want to kill the local librarian?

Everyone was talking about suspect #1: Chuck.

Alan Graham's friend Bud Bernhard said Ruth told him that she was in fear for her life—from her son.

Why? Did she sense that his financial desperation and volatile temper would lead to violent behavior? Did she understand how much trauma he had suffered from the shock treatments? Neighbors who heard their shouting matches could certainly vouch for the visceral hatred between these two.

Indeed, the dirt on Chuck was that he had spent time in mental hospitals. And Ruth was vocal about her problems with Chuck—with her friends, with her brother and with anyone who was within earshot.

Standing in line at the post office— where she most likely was waiting to mail Chuck's monthly allowance "promptly," as he demanded—Esky heard her yell, "My son Charles! You have no idea the troubles of my life!" And she stormed out the door, slamming it behind her.

Though many of Chuck's friends had cut ties with him, Esky and her husband, John, stayed in close touch with him over the years—though Esky found him difficult to tolerate. Gidget-pretty, Esky was raised in Coronado, spending her teenage years with Chuck on the beach. "People ask me if Chuck did it. I'm pretty sure he didn't, but I'm not sure. You know what I mean?"

Esky Wallace Kurtz, childhood friend of Chuck Quinn's, on the Coronado beach with her dog. *Esky Kurtz.*

One thing Esky knew for sure: Chuck was forever altered by the shock treatments his mother had subjected him to when he returned from Tahiti. John Elwell says his mind was "fried" from the treatments. And Chuck deeply resented Ruth for it. But would he have killed over it?

Others around town pointed fingers at the jewel thieves.

One of the pastors at Sacred Heart, Father John Wheeler, said a woman in confession claimed one of the Cameo Bandits committed the murder.

Alan Graham told his friends that he was sure the cops were going to accuse him of the crime, even though he said he had not done it. But he told them *he* could solve the mystery. He said he had a hunch who did it. Was he bluffing? Or did he know who killed Ruth Quinn?

Once the Cameo Bandits served their sentences, they were most likely back on the island, roaming around Coronado. At least Alan Graham was. Did he hold a grudge against Ruth for testifying against him and ensuring his conviction? He had an alibi for the evening of the murder. But could he have *arranged* to have her killed?

Coronado is a small town, where everyone knows everyone else's business—and their routines. And Ruth had a predictable one.

In the winter of 1975, she took a walk and attended Mass every morning. During Lent, she often also attended the evening church service. She served with the Altar Society at Sacred Heart, cleaning the Holy Water fountains several times a week. She volunteered at the Coronado Hospital six nights a month, delivering flowers and checking in visitors. She gave lectures on opera in the local schools. Sometimes, she went to the grocery store or the pharmacy or the library. Occasionally, she had lunch or dinner with friends.

Otherwise, she stayed home. Two neighbors came to visit her after school. Little Michael and Jimmy Callahan, seven and eight, charmed her. They must have reminded her of Chuck and Michael. "Mrs. Quinn was just a huge part of our life," Michael remembered. With their parents recently divorced and their mother working to make ends meet, the two boys visited Ruth until their mother came home from work. She was not their babysitter: "She was my friend." Just like Michael, Ruth was an avid reader, and "she talked to us like adults." She had a big color television, a rarity in the 1970s, and she shared the candy packages she received on a quarterly basis from the Heide Candy Company. Michael and Jimmy visited Ruth every day, except for Saturdays, when Ruth spent the morning listening to opera.

Sitting on her patio with the boys, her books and the birds singing lustily, she eagerly anticipated the arrival of spring. It had been a long winter.

Ruth (*left*) and Hank (*right*) at the wedding of Valerie Quate, the daughter of Laura Christian, circa 1960s. In the latter part of her life, Ruth never looked happy in photos. *Valerie Quate.*

Ruth's little cottage was cozy, but it was drafty. She complained that it was "one board thick" and without adequate heat.

Winters in Coronado were not frigid—at least not by East Coast standards. But Southern Californians have thin skin. If the temperature dips below fifty degrees at night—as it frequently does in the winter months—everyone dusts off their ski parkas. And winter *is* the rainy season, when downpours are frequent. The storms leave a damp chill in the air—both inside and out.

In her last letter to Chuck, two weeks before she was murdered, Ruth shivered during the short days of the Southern California winter: "I am glad the winter is almost over! And it has been wintry in this house. February was the coldest since 1916, the weather man said."

Ruth's cottage was also vulnerable—at least from a security standpoint. The long driveway was dark at night, and in 1975, security cameras were not common. After the burglary, Ruth installed a porch light and Hank put a lock on the door to his bedroom. It was not actually his bedroom. Ruth still tried to preserve it for Chuck, but Hank *did* sleep there several nights a week. Could he have also stored a gun in that locked bedroom?

He could have, but none of the locals suspected Hank had shot his sister. He seemed too fragile, too mild-mannered, too timid and too weak to be capable of such an act.

Law enforcement disagreed. Chuck was willing to feed that suspicion. He wrote a letter to Detective Paul Dodson in May 1975 with a host of "leads" he had collected for the detective's follow-up, including this one: "When I was in Coronado on Christmas Day 1974, which was the last time my mother and I were together, she said to me that she 'was afraid for her life.' When I asked her why, she responded that: 'it was because of things my brother had said in the community.'"

16

DEAD ENDS

We all thought Hank did it, but we could not find a gun.
—*Coronado police detective Paul Dodson*

On the afternoon of the murder, Hank broke his routine. Most days, he drove Lucinda to Ruth's house for dinner and then slept there. On Sunday, March 16, he walked. Two young boys noticed him arriving on foot. That was unusual. Unfortunately, their eyewitness accounts were dismissed, almost certainly because they were minors.

The boys lived with their family across the street from Ruth at 500 Pomona Avenue. The street was a good place to skateboard. It was flat, and the sidewalks curved gently but not sharply. Charlie and Bill White, eleven and twelve years old, respectively, were outside practicing their hobby that Sunday afternoon in the hours before *The Wonderful World of Disney*. That night, "Deacon, the High-Noon Dog" aired. Charlie was freckled with braces, and Bill was tall and lanky. Both boys had bangs hanging over their eyes, often wore striped T-shirts and probably sported Vans sneakers and long socks, outfits popular with the skateboarders of the 1970s.

Around 4:15 p.m., they noticed Hank Leyendecker walking north toward Ruth's cottage. That was odd. Not the visit—Hank ate dinner at Ruth's house several evenings a week, and he slept there most nights. They were accustomed to seeing him pop in and out. He usually drove Lucinda, and everyone knew where he was if they spotted Lucinda. Why was Hank coming to Ruth's house on foot?

Skateboarders Charlie and Bill White in their Coronado Middle School yearbooks. The eleven- and twelve-year-old brothers lived across the street from Ruth's home. *Coronado Public Library.*

They watched as he entered Ruth's residence. They never saw him leave. And they were skateboarding outside until 8:00 p.m.

In fact, no one saw Hank again until he returned to Laura Christian's house for dinner. She said he arrived at her home between 6:30 and 7:00 p.m.

Anyone coming to Ruth's house by car had to, and still must, drive down a narrow driveway off Pomona Avenue. It is a dead end, so drivers must turn around and exit the same way they arrived. Someone arriving on foot, however, had two options: to walk down the driveway *or* approach from behind the house, by slipping between two homes on Glorietta. Any pedestrian *leaving* the scene on foot would have the same two options.

Chief LeBlanc started questioning Hank at the crime scene. When did he last see Ruth? Around 10:00 a.m., before Sunday morning Mass. Where was he this afternoon? At Laura's house having a late lunch. Then what? Well, he went to the Millers. Hank had rented an alley suite from the couple since his mother died in 1957, but he rarely spent time in it.

His routine was to go to Ruth's for dinner and spend the night. He said she prepared an early dinner on Sundays so she could eat while watching her favorite TV programs. Hank usually joined her. But the day of the murder, he went to Laura's for dinner instead. Why? Did the police ask him why he changed his routine that day?

Then what did he do?

At 10:00 p.m., he said to police, he told Laura he was heading to Ruth's for the night.

When did he arrive at 511 Pomona? Well, Hank alleged, he arrived at the house at 10:15 or 10:20 p.m. He noticed that the porch light was not on, which was unusual. Using his key to enter the house, he noticed the kitchen and bedroom lights were on. And the TV was blaring. This, too, was unusual. "Ruth?" he called out. No response. Entering the rear bedroom, he found her lying on her bed. "Ruth!" he called out again, as he shook her. "I thought she had had a heart attack." Why would he say that, with blood on her face and hand, bloody sheets and a pillow with bullet holes next to her?

Was Hank emotional about his sister's death? Traumatized by the experience of finding the body? The police wanted to know. Shocked and sad is what Laura Christian's daughter Valerie Quate remembers.

Hank was called to the station for further questioning.

When Hank arrived for his interview, Detective Dodson was ready. He was convinced Hank was guilty. The murder seemed like the clumsy work of an old man. After all, it took two shots to do the job.

Dodson questioned him: "I tried to trip him up. He told me he had learned about weapons at the Wyoming dude ranch. When I repeated it back to him, I inserted the [gun type]. He corrected me and told me, 'I didn't say that.'"

Asked if he would take a polygraph test, Hank refused and referred Detective Dodson to his attorney, Lowell Davies. Hank advised his girlfriend Laura to refuse questioning as well.

Interviewed on the patio at Panera's in Coronado in 2021, Dodson remembered the case well. He had focused his investigation on Hank immediately. Although he retired from the police force in 1986, Dodson stayed in Coronado, working for the next six years as director of security for the Coronado Shores, the large high-rise beachfront condominium community sandwiched between the Hotel del and the Navy SEAL compound. Now fully retired, Dodson and his wife have remained active volunteers in the community that he served for so long.

Ballistics tests revealed that the weapon used was either an Arminius Titan Tiger .38 caliber or a .357 Magnum. A .357 Magnum seems unlikely. Given the caliber's power, the gun would have left a much messier crime scene.

One of the first things Dodson did was to obtain a printout of all registered owners of this type of gun in San Diego County. "The stack was a foot high. It went nowhere."

Hank told Dodson that Alan Graham's friend Bud Bernhard had left a note on Hank's car with advice: "Look to motive." What did he mean? Who wanted Ruth dead?

Was Hank pointing the finger at his nephew? Forty-two-year-old Chuck was always in need of money and seemed to think his family had some. Chuck, the prodigal son, publicly claimed he knew nothing about an inheritance. He hated his mother. He *was* the obvious suspect.

But Chuck had an alibi in Dr. Pat Flynn, who vouched that Chuck had been a houseguest at their home in Carson City. However, he was unaware of Chuck's whereabouts all day on Sunday, March 16, as Chuck had been gone most of the day Ruth was murdered, hiking or skiing with a friend. But, Pat joked, "He would have needed a Phantom fighter jet to get to Coronado and back." In truth, it would have taken Chuck about nine hours to drive to Coronado and another nine hours to drive back to Carson City.

As soon as Chuck arrived in Coronado on March 18, even before Ruth was buried, police asked to speak to him. He agreed to sit down for an interview. This is when he realized he *was* suspect #1. With the tape recorder running, law enforcement officers asked probing questions, and he got scared, later saying, "You know we grow up thinking that police are our friends and it's not always the case. It's not always the case at all. Their job is to put somebody in jail. They're not interested in whether you're guilty or not guilty. That's another department—the courts. The role of the police department is to arrest somebody and lock them up, and so that was their focus."

Like Hank, he refused to take a polygraph test. Chuck feared the test itself for several reasons. "It is well documented that persons with *very sensitive* consciones [sic] who are ultra aware of their behavior often score a false positive on polygraph tests," he alleged. This is what he tried to explain to police detectives in Coronado. "I objected to the use of a *machine* to determine innocence or guilt verses [sic] the decision of a jury. There is the 'Big Brother' aspect of the government use of the polygraph which is a violation of personal privacy and dignity. It therefore should be outlawed from use in the U.S. judicial system."

Casting about for motives and offenders and to deflect attention from himself, Chuck pointed to his mother's maid. What about Evelyn? Chuck wondered. Were she and Ruth on good terms?

The police interviewed all of Ruth's neighbors. There was the Parker and Callahan extended family, who owned Ruth's cottage and several other properties on that block. They told a strange story: their grandmother had made a day trip to the island on Sunday, March 16. Ruth's landlord, she was the one who came by Sunday afternoon to inspect the leaky roof Ruth was complaining about. She drove into town in a new Mercedes. When Chuck arrived two days later, he commented on the Mercedes to the Callahan family. They wondered: How did he know about their grandmother's new car?

Police interviewed another neighbor, Ezra Parker, a World War II Navy veteran who had survived the sinking of the aircraft carrier USS *Hornet* during the Battle of Midway. He lived behind Ruth at 520 Glorietta and was the brother of Ruth's landlady. He had guns. According to the police, all were .22 caliber. His son Michael Parker suffered from schizophrenia and had escaped from probation camp on March 14. Where was he on March 16?

Ezra's whereabouts that afternoon were also unclear. His sister-in-law thought he might have gone down to Ruth's. Maybe he was inspecting the leaky roof? She sent a teen to look for him there.

There was no answer when that teenager, Joe Ditler, knocked on Ruth's door. Tall and lean, with a mop of shaggy hair and a face full of freckles, Ditler was an avid surfer and tennis player and made friends with all the Coronado old-timers on the courts and in the surf, including Hank and Ezra.

The television was blaring, so Joe was pretty sure someone was home. He knocked even louder, so loud that the next-door neighbor's dog started barking. Putting his ear to the door, all he heard was the TV. He shrugged and left.

Louis Niles, who lived at 522 Glorietta, claimed he heard gunshots between 6:45 and 7:00 p.m. Why didn't he call the police? Would living near a military base desensitize you to the sound of gunshots? And why didn't any other neighbors in that tightly packed block of homes hear or report hearing gunshots?

Wagging tongues suspected Chuck, Chuck suspected his mother's maid, Detective Dodson suspected Hank. Who did Hank suspect? Alan Graham.

But what would be Alan's motive? Revenge for being caught stealing her cameos? Three years later?

"The murder scared him," his former brother-in-law, Andy Morrison, remembered. "He did not want to get deported." Alan was nervous. He asked Andy to sit with him when the police questioned him. His alibi? He had been with his wife at a dinner party all evening on March 16.

And what about his previous crime against Ruth? He was truly remorseful, he claimed. "I sent her a letter of apology and a book of poems, from jail," he told police earnestly. Surely they did not believe that he was capable of killing another human being?

17

TRY SPENDING THAT
IN A TOMB

The next morning, they found her in the kitchen with her legs up like a dead fucking cockroach. And she got all of it, but you try spending that in the tomb, bitch. And that's that.
—*Alan Graham, in a podcast interview, 2022*

About a year before Ruth's death, in April 1974, Alan Graham was connected to another suspicious death that made headlines: that of Jim Morrison's longtime girlfriend Pamela Courson.

Pamela was discovered—not in the kitchen, as Alan Graham alleged—but on the living room couch in the house of friends where she was staying. Her hosts thought the red-haired waif was napping until they discovered she was not breathing. She died of a heroin overdose.

She had been wandering aimlessly through life since Jim's untimely death three years prior, in 1971. In a constant state of grief and shock, Pamela found solace in new lovers, opiates and painkillers, all while she couch-surfed with friends in Los Angeles and the Bay Area. Sometimes, late at night, she called Jim's brother, Andy. Once she asked if he would have a baby with her. She wanted a child with Jim's DNA.

Although she and Jim were not legally married, she called herself "Pamela Morrison." She wanted to be recognized, legally, as Jim's common-law wife in the eyes of the public and, especially, the courts.

Jim had named her his sole heir in a will drawn up in 1969. If she died, the will stipulated, Jim's estate was to be divided equally between Jim's brother, Andy, and sister, Anne.

The will took years to adjudicate. While it was held up in legal battles, Pamela was broke. She sold her clothing boutique that Jim had purchased for her. She sold many of his possessions. She filed a "declaration in support of a widow's allowance," asking for his estate to provide her an interim monthly allowance.

At the same time, the Doors' surviving band members were suing Jim's estate for repayment of large cash advances they said were paid to him. The estate seemed to be eternally tied up in court. Nonstop litigation dominated Pamela's life and her fragile hold on it for the next three years.

Alan Graham, married to Jim's sister, Anne, deeply resented Pamela. She did not inform the Morrison family of Jim's sudden death in Paris. They and Alan heard it from the media. He did not believe her version of events: that she found Jim dead in a bathtub in their apartment. Alan was outraged that Pamela had told the Paris authorities that Jim had no family. And it saddened them all that she had quickly and quietly buried him far from home, in Paris at the Père Lachaise Cemetery, a famous resting place for poets and artists like Frédéric Chopin, Oscar Wilde and Marcel Proust. They were not given an opportunity to attend the burial, witnessed by only five people. No autopsy was performed. The official cause of death was heart failure.

Jim was under the ground and Pamela back in the United States before the world woke up to the fact that the Lizard King was gone.

Alan believed Pamela was responsible for Jim's death. He was convinced that she—or one of her friends—provided him a lethal dose of heroin that killed the singer.

He opined, "Eve tempted Adam and said, 'Listen, never had better sex than this in your life when you take a little hit of this.'" Mixed with alcohol, he alleged, the outcome was deadly.

Alan called Pamela with veiled threats: "I know what you did." He warned her that bad karma was now following her.

Pamela was recognized by the courts as Jim's common-law wife in April 1974. But she, too, turned up dead soon thereafter from a heroin overdose. Pamela's parents, Corky and Penny Courson, were suspicious. They wanted the death investigated as a murder. Her apartment had been broken into during her memorial service and several of Jim's personal possessions had been stolen. And her autopsy report revealed no evidence of chronic heroin use: "The examination of the skin only disclosed the one fresh injection site, and there was no evidence of acute or external trauma."

The Coursons could not accept Pamela's death as an overdose of her own doing. They pointed their fingers at Alan. They knew he had harassed her with phone calls and claimed he had threatened Pamela just one week before her death. Alan said the Coursons tried to get him indicted for Pamela's murder, but there clearly was not enough evidence.

Could Alan have given Pamela a "hotshot" of heroin? Why did he insist Pamela was found in the kitchen with her legs up in the air "like a dead fucking cockroach"? Was he hoping for a payout from Jim's estate if Pamela was dead? And, if he did not kill her, could this lifelong thief have been responsible for the break-in of her apartment?

Pamela had no will. Her parents were deemed the beneficiaries. But because she successfully attained status as Jim's common-law wife, Admiral and Mrs. Morrison were later able to successfully petition for part of her inheritance. In 1979, the court awarded the Morrisons half of it.

The popularity of the Doors exploded after Jim's death, and he amassed a cult following, one that has not dissipated over time. When the song "The End" haunted the opening scene of the film *Apocalypse Now* in 1979, a new generation of fans was introduced to the music. A controversial biography of Morrison and the history of the Doors called *No One Here Gets Out Alive* was published in 1980. The surviving members of the band, the Courson family and the Morrison family did not like it, but fans did. The book sold more than two million copies. In 1981, the band released a "greatest hits" album, and it instantly hit the Billboard Top 10. That same year, *Rolling Stone* magazine featured a cover image of Jim Morrison with the headline: "He's hot, he's sexy and he's dead." When a new anthology of his work was published by the estate, with previously unpublished excerpts from his private diaries, it included rare photographs and his last poetry recording. It instantly hit the *New York Times* bestseller list—in 2021.

Admiral and Mrs. Morrison spent their sunset years like many retired naval officers, in their home in Coronado. Jim's gold records hung on the wall. They were active socially on the island and had a large set of friends who all said the couple never spoke publicly about their son.

When Admiral Morrison died in 2008, their half of Jim's estate passed to the Morrisons' surviving children, Andy and Anne. By that time, Anne and her husband, Alan Graham, were divorced. Alan probably never was able to tap into the significant royalties, nor was he ever successful in capitalizing on his familial relationship. But he spent a lifetime trying. He remained on the margins—in Hollywood, in Coronado society and within the Morrison family—until he began working with *Hustler*'s Larry Flynt in the 1980s.

18

CAPTAIN PINK

The most dangerous adventure I ever went on in my life was Springfield, Missouri.
—Alan Graham

A lan Graham had a knack for meeting famous people. When Prince Charles, then serving in the Royal Navy, paid a visit to Coronado in 1974, he wanted a surf lesson from locals. Robert Duryea, owner of the island surf shop DuRay's, obliged. Captured in the *Coronado Journal*, there was Alan grinning with Duryea, the NAS North Island commanding officer and the prince.

He had a habit of ingratiating himself with celebrities and then hanging on—that is, until they figured out he was a con artist. "My parents hated him," his former brother-in-law Andy Morrison admitted. "But they put up with him because they loved my sister." Alan and Anne divorced in 1986, but he continued to drop the Morrison name when it could help him.

It worked for a while with Sylvester Stallone, who hired Alan and his construction crew to work on his house and then to babysit his son Sage. When Stallone discovered that Alan was Jim Morrison's brother-in-law, "Stallone listened to my every word and in the process swallowed the bait, the hook, the line, the pole, and half my arm." According to Alan, Stallone engaged Alan to serve as an intermediary between Stallone and Admiral and Mrs. Morrison. Stallone wanted to get access to movie rights to make a film about Jim Morrison and the Doors. Alan wanted a piece of the pie.

Stallone was not the only one in Hollywood trying to make a movie about the Doors. John Travolta, Francis Ford Coppola and Martin Scorsese—among many others—were interested in buying the rights from the estate. Alan acted like he was the gateway to the deal.

And it was probably how Alan crossed paths with Larry Flynt, the embattled founder of *Hustler* magazine and Hustler TV, the biggest name in porn in the 1980s. He often used constitutional protections of freedom of speech to defend his lucrative business ventures—even if they graphically exploited women.

Over the Christmas holidays in 1983, Larry Flynt was making headlines again, this time from behind bars at a government medical detention center in Springfield, Missouri, following a bizarre appearance in court, where Flynt—confined to a wheelchair after being shot by a sniper in 1978—showed up wearing a diaper made of an American flag. Sent against his will to Springfield, there he was ordered to have a mental competency evaluation.

Protesting what he alleged was "cruel and unusual punishment" and claiming he was poisoned there, Flynt embarked on a hunger strike from inside the prison.

Enter Alan Graham, who was determined to make headlines and money with Flynt. He became Flynt's self-styled spokesman and gained a lot of publicity for himself. How did Alan get hooked up with Flynt? Could Alan have promised access to the Morrisons and potential movie rights for a film about his dead brother-in-law?

However the introduction was made, Alan went to "work" for Larry Flynt. In protest over the government's medical treatment—or lack thereof—of Flynt, Alan and several other Flynt supporters invaded Springfield, Missouri, over several weeks.

The group of pranksters called themselves the "Flyntstones." Still married to the Morrisons' daughter, Anne, and now the father of three young children, Alan went by the alias "Captain Pink." Captain Pink and the Flyntstones were intent on shaking up the conservative and sober city of Springfield, home to the U.S. Assemblies of God and a Baptist Bible college.

Decked out in pink tights, a pink cape, pink shoes, a pink mask, a pink baby Jesus and a toy sword, he arrived in Springfield with a suitcase of cash and a brainstorm of planned pranks. "We flew in every lunatic, misfit, criminal and every other character so we could expand our three-ring circus," Alan recalled.

Alan was the ringleader and organized their escapades: "We terrorized the community," Alan bragged, "turning it upside down." To garner headlines, the Flyntstones stood outside the prison with "Free Flynt" signs; they ran through hotel hallways in the middle of the night in pink regalia; they jumped from a second-story balcony yelling, "Bonzai!"; and they closed down the bars with local college kids. They unsuccessfully petitioned to rename a street "Flyntstone Avenue." And they ran out of town with the prison warden's daughter, whom Alan "married" in a mock wedding ceremony.

The capers ended when Flynt was released from Fed Med, and Alan went home to Coronado. Here, he was back in the shadows again until he could find a way to drum up more publicity for himself.

Ultimately, the deal for a movie about the Doors was secured by Oliver Stone, who produced a blockbuster film in 1991. Alan got himself hired as a consultant. His second wife and children were extras. This generated a little bit of media coverage for him and perpetuated his claim to be the only one alive who truly knew the real Jim Morrison—even though Alan has never produced one photo of Jim and Alan together.

In January 2009, Alan finally produced the memoir on Jim Morrison that he had promised for decades to write, a self-published tome titled *I Remember Jim Morrison Too*. "It chronicles a lot about Jim Morrison but mostly about my adventures here in America, the aftereffects of Jim Morrison, the people I met…and the doors I answered because I was Jim Morrison's brother-in-law and for no other reason. Once I got inside, my skills took the floor, and I took advantage of every single relationship I ever had."

19

A CROSS TO BEAR

Chuck should have stuck to sex and waves...like us.
—*John Elwell, on surfing, carousing and Chuck Quinn, 2004*

D r. Pat Flynn answered the phone in January 1981 at his home in Carson City, Nevada, and was surprised to learn that the voice on the other end of the line was calling from the Marin County, California sheriff's office. They had some questions about Chuck Quinn.

Captain Flynn was a Navy doctor stationed in Fallon, Nevada, and a Beach Boys lookalike, with broad shoulders and slicked-back hair. He had a boxer's nose, although it was broken in a car accident, not in the ring. He was still commuting one hundred miles from his home in Carson City, where he chose to raise his family. Pat had known Chuck for decades. His wife, Marion, and their children had hiked and camped with Chuck. He had been a guest in their home many times, including the weekend his mother had been murdered. And Pat Flynn had provided the police with that crucial alibi for Chuck.

The caller wanted to know details about Chuck Quinn and his hiking habits. Among other things.

Why?

For twenty-one months in 1980 and 1981, the Bay Area community had been terrorized by a serial killer, a man who stalked and killed hikers on Mount Tamalpais in Marin County. He was called the Trailside Killer. The victims were found raped and shot with a .38-caliber pistol—the same caliber pistol probably used to kill Ruth.

A team of psychologists had developed a profile of the killer: a handsome man with a full head of hair, between the age of twenty-eight and thirty-five, personable and not intimidating to his victims.

The drawing looked a little bit like Chuck.

The Marin County Sheriff's Department wanted to know: What were his hiking habits *now*?

Chuck was a regular hiker and had traversed many mountains on foot—as well as on skis.

In the Bay Area, he did take walks on Mount Tamalpais. Almost fifty years old, Chuck was still a handsome and physically fit man. In addition to hiking, he was still skiing and running and sailing. And he had recently taken up rowing in the Bay, joining the South End Rowing Club.

He was still living off the estate he had inherited from his mother six years prior, and he was trying to make it last. His friend Esky Kurtz's husband, John, gave him pointers on the stock market.

Pious, he attended Mass almost daily, and he volunteered with Mother Teresa's Missionaries of Charity in the city and with incarcerated alcoholics in San Quentin Prison in Marin County.

Fervently religious, he briefly toyed with the idea of becoming a Jesuit priest, but he was not celibate. And his checkered history with women and the children he fathered but did not raise might have disqualified him. Mother Clarke had also told him his temperament was not suited to fulfill the vow of obedience.

But he was determined to "live in the presence of Jesus," as he termed it. Fortunately, this presented few obstacles in finding women companions.

He still lived in the same modest studio apartment in San Francisco and was as fastidious in his housekeeping as his mother and uncle were. His home and possessions were almost surgically antiseptic, clean and shiny with crisp white monogrammed towels in the bathroom, his brushes and combs neatly arranged in a line.

Yet paradoxically, Chuck was also becoming a pack rat, and in the thirty years he lived in this apartment in the city, he never seemed to throw away a single piece of paper. Boxes and boxes of letters, notes, journal entries, bank statements, newspaper articles, family documents and photographs—all date-stamped—started to accumulate in the corners of his apartment.

He traveled when he could, to ski and surf and hike, usually by train. Chuck had a lifelong childlike fascination with trains. Unfortunately, he had to avoid Utah—or at least keep a low profile there—because of the state's "bastardry law," where he could be caught and subject to fines for failure to pay child support for his first child.

He was planning a hike to Mount Whitney and probably trained on the local mountains in preparation. But, since the news of the murders had hit the media, he was avoiding Mount Tam.

Then his old Coronado friend Pat Flynn called about these murders that were frightening Marin County residents.

Pat had spent a long time pondering this call. Should he tell Chuck what the Marin County sheriffs had asked him? Should he share their line of questioning and its invasive nature?

Pat and Chuck had a common Achilles' heel: they were both recovering alcoholics. Pat credited Chuck for guiding him toward AA and the sober way of life: One Day at a Time. He had tremendous empathy for Chuck and all the tragedy he had suffered in his life. What should he do?

The intelligence Pat gleaned from the line of questioning was incendiary. But he and Chuck had a bond that AA members could appreciate. There was mutual respect, care and confidentiality.

So, he picked up the phone and called Chuck in San Francisco.

"I weighed carefully whether or not to call you," Pat admitted. "I didn't want to upset you or make you paranoid."

"You did the right thing, Pat," Chuck reassured him, "to always keep the lines of communication open."

Pat relayed all the gory details: the sheriff's office wanted to know more about Ruth Quinn's murder and Chuck's alibi, which Pat provided once more—using an old 1975 calendar he still kept. They asked about Chuck's sex life and attitudes toward women. They probed into his mental breakdown in Tahiti, his subsequent hospitalization and his current mental health. They inquired about Chuck's gun use and hunting experience—and details of his hiking habits.

"I protested their line of questioning, Chuck," Pat said, indignantly. "I called it an invasion of privacy."

Chuck took the news calmly. He said that he had been watched and investigated so often in his life that he was becoming accustomed to it.

Sadly and soberly, Chuck responded, "This is my cross to bear, Pat."

20

FINDING DEAD BODIES

Killing is easier the second time around.
—*Sergeant Bob Paseman, former Coronado police officer*

Hank's life after Ruth died was much as before. He played a lot of tennis and took long drives around San Diego County in Lucinda. He still had the strong and sturdy gait of an athlete, but his mannerisms and whiny, nasal voice gave away his advancing age. After decades of sun worshipping, he was plagued with skin cancer, suffering through multiple surgeries to remove the cancerous lesions and graft skin from various places on his body to keep his face intact. It was not pretty.

And he spent very little of his own money. He rarely reached for the bill when he and his tennis partners decamped to La Avenida restaurant for lunch after a vigorous match.

He was still dating Laura Christian, but he did not spend much money on her, either. They had a routine to their dating life. It was a bit unconventional, but it seemed to work for them. Laura took over Ruth's role of cooking for Hank several nights a week. And on the other nights, they would go out to dinner. To avoid paying for expensive restaurant cocktails, Hank would load the Jack Daniels into Lucinda, pick up Laura and head to their island restaurant favorites, the Chart House or Mulvaney's, for dinner. There, sitting in the car in the parking lot, they would enjoy happy hour.

Happy hour was followed by dinner, where Hank inspected the bill closely. Because Laura usually had too many drinks, dinner was soon followed by bedtime for Laura. Hank would gently tuck "Little Laura" into bed. As Laura's daughter Valerie attested, "He loved her." Afterward, he sometimes went back to his rented room at the Millers' home on B Avenue or to the apartment he later rented at Oakwood Apartments, the low-rise complex where many single people on the island lived.

After decades together, Hank and Laura were planning to move closer to each other—if not in the same home. Laura was renovating a small ancillary building in her backyard. Her son Kemp worked in construction and was converting it into a small casita with a bedroom and bathroom for Hank. After thirty years of dating, it would have been the closest they ever came to living together.

This type of structure would have been and still is common in Coronado. Estimates are that a full one-third of Coronado's eighteen thousand residents lives in these alley homes or "granny flats," as the locals call them. Converted garages, apartments above garages, cabanas and patio homes—all built behind street-front homes, with their own "1/2" addresses—line every alley on the island. Some even have their own parking space, patio and patch of grass. With near-perfect weather year-round, most residents don't need much indoor space. They can live outside most of the days and evenings.

For Hank, this casita that Laura was building for him was an act of true love. Even though he could afford his own place, she was offering space at hers. He would never move in because Little Laura died.

Too many drinks over too many years took their toll. On the morning of February 6, 1980, Hank let himself into her home. He told police that he called out her name. Silence.

He searched the house. Opening the door to her bathroom, he said, he found her in the bathtub, unresponsive. She was dead, at fifty-seven, from alcohol poisoning. She had probably been dead since the night before. This time, he called the Coronado police first.

When they arrived, the officers were surprised to find Hank at the scene of another dead body.

They chided him. "You again?"

Hank seemed offended.

At the funeral for her mother at Sacred Heart, Valerie Quate stood outside greeting guests. One friend came up and revealed with a smirk on her face, "I know why your mom died. It's because Hank was going to move in with her."

Valerie smiled wanly and admitted, "I thought the same thing."

21

LET SLEEPING DOGS LIE

I expect great things of you: to be big and strong, to be bright and helpful and
above all to love your dear mother.
—*Charles Quinn in his first letter to his son, Chuck, 1934*

In the years after Ruth's death, Chuck made occasional visits to Coronado, especially around the Fourth of July. The midsummer holiday celebration was one of the best times of the year to be on the island.

The city hosts an iconic patriotic parade every year on Independence Day. Participants march down more than a dozen blocks along Orange Avenue, which bisects the island. A median in the middle of the avenue serves as an ideal viewing venue. The procession features homemade floats, beauty queens, Clydesdales, veterans from World War II and the Korean War and the Vietnam War, Boy Scouts, politicians in convertibles, cheerleaders, marching bands and Shriners. Lots of Shriners. Spectators stake out their spot starting at 5:00 a.m.

Runners of all ages tour the island in an early morning 5K, Navy SEAL "Leapfrogs" parachute onto the golf course that afternoon and fireworks light up the San Diego Bay as soon as the sun sets. Picnics and barbecues are held around the village. Bonfires attract crowds of teenagers all evening at Central Beach. And it is on this holiday that Coronado High School hosts its annual homecoming party for all CHS alumni.

Chuck did not go to Coronado High School, even though he wanted to attend with his friends. Over his protests, Ruth instead sent him to

Eight women, dressed in crown-themed outfits, marching side by side in the parade, July 4, 1971. Each woman is carrying a pole banner to spell out the word CORONADO. *Tommy Lark Photograph Collection; Coronado Public Library.*

Villanova Preparatory School, a boys Catholic boarding school in Ojai, California.

Coming home to Coronado for the all-class reunion party at the golf course gave him a chance to catch up with childhood friends like John Elwell, Tom Carlin, Tom Keck, Pike Meade, Ted Johnson and Mike Moret. He usually overstayed his welcome at their homes and sometimes he gave their young daughters too much attention. But these friends still tolerated him.

On one occasion, he showed up at night, unannounced, at the home of his old friend and former neighbor Dick Tarbuck, who had been there when Chuck's brother was run over and killed by a truck back in 1939. When Chuck knocked on Dick's door, it was after 9:30 p.m. and dark. The two had not seen each other in decades. Dick was startled, but Chuck said he wanted to catch up. "I didn't invite him inside," Dick admitted, "because I had heard stories about his erratic behavior." Instead, they sat on the patio and talked. Neither one brought up the painful memory of little Michael's death.

While in town, Chuck would usually spend time with his uncle Hank.

Chuck was trying to repair his relationship with his mother's brother. Like most of his family relationships, it was fraught with conflict. Visits ended in flared tempers and hostile words, not unlike the way his visits with his mother deteriorated.

Chuck and Hank were both trying to even out their interactions, smooth things over, make amends and tamp down the raging emotions that flared in their souls and sparked their family fights. They still resented each other. And they still resembled each other: both were eccentric, fastidious and frugal, living off family inheritance, unemployed and plagued by intermittent mental illness.

But the two were the only immediate family each had left. And Hank was the only consistent adult male figure in Chuck's life. He was not much of a paternal figure. But he was all Chuck had.

In July 1984, during one of those extended stays Chuck made on the island, Hank and Chuck were having a leisurely visit when the topic of conversation drifted to Ruth and who had killed her.

Hank was adamant. "I'm certain [Alan] Graham did it." Hank was convinced that the harassing phone calls that forced Ruth to privatize her phone number came from Alan or his family. He believed Alan's history of criminal behavior was inherited: "I'm told by members of the Coronado Police Department that Graham's father was one of the most notorious con men in England." How would the police know this rumor? And it *was* only a rumor. And why would the police share information like this with Hank?

Content that the case was dormant, Hank advised Chuck that night not to stir the pot: "Let sleeping dogs lie. Ruth wanted to die. She wanted to go to Rosecrans."

It was a chilling statement. Is this how he rationalized her murder?

Just a few months later, in November 1984, Hank was admitted to Coronado Hospital for another round of routine surgery to remove more cancerous lesions from his face. Dutifully, Chuck came to visit. Mere hours after Chuck left on a plane bound for home in San Francisco, Hank was dead. According to several sources, Chuck was the last person to see Hank alive. Some townsfolk found that coincidence suspicious.

Hank's stinginess paid off: he had $78,000 in his checking account when he died and the rest of the trust he had inherited from his mother invested in securities.

Chuck was expecting to inherit *something* from Hank. No such luck. Hank instead gave his money to charities and to Laura Christian's children and grandchildren.

The Heide family mausoleum in Calvary Cemetery, Queens, New York, where Hank Leyendecker chose to be buried. *Quinn family.*

Was Chuck disappointed that Hank left him nothing? If he was, he pretended it did not matter to him. In fact, Chuck claimed many times that money was never important to him. "I grew up thinking that I was rich because my grandmother lived at the hotel and we had all of our parties up there—Christmas and New Year's and Thanksgiving—and all of our birthday parties." He was dazzled by all those shiny objects. As a kid, "You're seeing life through a clouded lens." But it was a myth. "As we get older, that clears and we begin to see what truth is, if we're lucky, and if we are honest."

In the end, "All I wanted was his belt buckle." Ah yes, the shiny silver belt buckle Hank the dude wore on his cowboy costume when he was at Eatons' Ranch. That coveted possession went to Laura's family, who managed Hank's estate.

And what about Lucinda?

Hank bequeathed her to his dermatologist, Dr. Ron Goldman. Goldman sent his brother Rodger and his nurse Deena Jones-Webber to retrieve the car. "We decided to drive it around Coronado and took a cruise by the beach," she remembered. Lucinda was a great car for cruising. "Halfway down Ocean Boulevard, these Jujyfruit balloons came floating over from behind the back seat and scared the crud out of me. Rodger said it was Hank's way of saying, 'Hi ho Miss Deena!'"

22

WHERE'S THE GUN?

I spent eleven and a half years as chief. We had four homicides.
Three were solved.
—Former Coronado police chief Art LeBlanc, 2004

D ecades after Ruth's death, Ruth's murder remained unsolved. Hank, suspect #2, was dead, having expired after his last cancer surgery in 1984. Chuck, suspect #1, was still living in the Bay Area, surviving off whatever was left of his inheritance and whatever odd jobs he could scrounge. Alan Graham, suspect #3, was raising a second family with his second wife in a small efficiency apartment in Coronado along the busy street that leads to the base on North Island.

The police involved in the case were retired. But they were still alive. What did they know?

While former Coronado police officer Sergeant Bob Paseman did not work on Ruth's case, he knew the victim and the suspects. He came to Coronado—like many people—with the Navy. He was an aviation hydraulics man at Naval Air Station Miramar in San Diego for almost four years. After a short stint with the phone company, he joined the Coronado Police Department. He still lives on the island. Paunchy, with a somewhat bulbous nose, moustache and sideburns, Sergeant Paseman fit the classic cop stereotype.

What was the Coronado Police Department like in the 1970s? "It was a joke. No one wanted to work or write tickets. And the ferry company paid the cops cash to divert traffic to the ferry—$40 a day." ($40 would be $234 in 2024 dollars.) They probably made more money with this side gig than they did with the department.

What did he remember about Ruth's investigation? Mostly how unprofessionally it began: "Chief LeBlanc went through the whole house. One of the sheriffs from San Diego couldn't believe they let LeBlanc walk all through the house. They never should have let him go through the scene." Paul Dodson echoed Paseman's complaint: "LeBlanc messed with the crime scene."

What did Chief LeBlanc remember?

The gated trailer park in Palm Desert where former Coronado police chief Art LeBlanc retired was tidy and manicured. His home was adorned with fake grass, plastic flowers and cacti. It had a two-car driveway and a small pool in the backyard. This was an upscale mobile home community. It was June 2004, and the desert air was hot and dry. Most residents were reclusive in the summertime, as were Chief LeBlanc and his wife.

Inside the brown-carpeted double-wide, Chief LeBlanc offered a seat at his kitchen table, while his wife watched game shows in her La-Z-Boy recliner. She was hooked up to an oxygen tank and sucking on a cigarette. The air inside was thicker than the air outside.

Chief LeBlanc was still portly, with a round face and a shiny pate. His eyes twinkled like Santa Claus, and he was surprisingly open about the cold case murder that had vexed him almost thirty years prior.

Before talking about the case of Ruth Quinn, however, Chief LeBlanc wanted to share details of his career. He was proud of it. He called himself a "cerebral cop"—part of a new generation of police that were better educated and open to innovation. His first beat was in Durbin, Michigan, but he soon made the move to California, because his wife suffered from asthma. Working in the police department in Signal Hill, near Long Beach, California, he hoped the ocean air and warm weather would help improve her health. It did not.

After she died, he never left California. And in 1969, he was selected by Coronado mayor Bob Wynn to become the island's police chief, beating out fifty other nominees. He was hired two months before the Coronado Bridge opened, which brought national media attention and many more outsiders to the island—outsiders who could now make a much quicker getaway than they could have on the ferry.

Coronado policing was a sleepy business before the bridge, with only a handful of crimes making the news. One of the most notorious was the case of the "Left Shoe Bandit." In the 1950s, a night stalker on the island was trailing women on their walks home. He would tackle them and pull from their feet one shoe, usually the left one. Then he would make a quick getaway, leaving his stunned victims on the ground. Sometimes, he would take advantage of unlocked doors and sneak into homes to steal more left shoes from women's closets.

After twenty months of multiple incidents all over the island and in other neighborhoods of San Diego, the thief was finally caught when he was chased out of a victim's home by her boyfriend. A fight erupted between the two men, police were called and the thief was arrested. He was a twenty-three-year-old naval aviator stationed at North Island. A search of his apartment turned up a collection of hundreds of stilettos, pumps and sandals. A plumber working in the bachelor officers' quarters at North Island, where the thief had once lived, found another cache of shoes hidden under a floor.

The case of the Shoe Bandit seems quaint by a measure of today's violent crimes, but it terrified Coronado women. And the criminal was a naval officer, a man who most in this military community expected to be of upstanding character. He was one of the island's own. That was even more disturbing. "He really did send a shock wave of fear through the community," said longtime resident Joe Ditler.

This is the same Joe Ditler who had the bad luck of being seen knocking on Ruth Quinn's door the day she was killed, which briefly made him a suspect. Joe came to Coronado with his parents in the 1960s, went to high school here and raised a family here. A lifelong and prolific writer and journalist who has made his living covering the waterways of San Diego and the history of Coronado, he has become the unofficial authority on the people and places of this island.

Joe nurtures friendships with Coronadans from all generations. Among the many people he has befriended over the years are Coronado police officers. These were men who mentored Joe and kept him out of trouble when he was a rebellious teenager.

As an adult, he has maintained many of these relationships, including with Chief LeBlanc. After LeBlanc left his job as the Coronado police chief, he went to work for the San Diego Harbor Police. Joe was a reporter for *The Log*, a newspaper covering the maritime industry.

Like any good reporter, Joe worked his sources on the waterfront. That included taking Chief LeBlanc out to lunch every now and then, where the old chief would drink heavily and brag. And at one memorable bayside lunch that included a cocktail or two, Joe turned the conversation to the topic of Ruth Quinn. "So," Joe said with his disarming and toothy grin, "Who killed her?"

Chief LeBlanc sighed and shook his head: "I don't know, Joe." But then, in a rare moment of disclosure, Chief LeBlanc leaned forward and, staring closely at Joe, confided: "But I know where the gun is." It was almost like he was teasing Joe. "It's in a safety deposit box." Here on the island? Yes.

Joe pressed him for more details. But LeBlanc raised his hands up in mock surrender and shook his head. He would share no more.

Now, in his trailer twenty years later, Chief LeBlanc was willing to talk again. The interview turned to the one murder his department did not solve on his watch. What about the confession he made to Joe Ditler two decades prior? Did he really know where the gun was?

Searching his memory, he recalled: "I can remember something about a safety deposit box." And who did Chief LeBlanc believe committed the crime? Chief LeBlanc narrowed his eyes and his focus on Hank. "I didn't like him," he admitted. "He was a loner."

23

THE TRAIL RUNS COLD

No suspects, no motive in Quinn killing.
—*Headline in the* Coronado Journal, *March 20, 1975*

C huck had a long to-do list on arriving in Coronado when his mother died. At the top of that list was getting a copy of Ruth's will. Where was it?

Close behind obtaining the will was getting into her safety deposit box at the Southern California First National Bank at 800 Orange Avenue. He met with Hank late in the evening on his first day in town to discuss the will and the safety deposit box. Did Hank have access to the box? Where was the will?

Chuck consulted several attorneys in the weeks following his mother's funeral about how and when he could view and inventory the contents of this box at the bank.

The detectives were also eager to search Ruth's safety deposit box. They obtained a search warrant to get access to it. They were hoping it might contain her will and life insurance policies, as well as some of the threatening letters Ruth had received since the cameo theft almost four years prior. All they found were securities certificates, jewelry, personal effects and appraisal documents.

The police finished their investigation of 511 Pomona about two weeks after Ruth's death, and Chuck was told he could enter the property at his discretion. He took a witness with him. Tearing off the hot pink police sticker that was taped over the entrance, he gingerly opened the door. The house looked much the same as it had over the Christmas holidays, when he claimed he had last visited the island and last seen Ruth.

Then he walked to her bedroom. It was eerie. The bloody sheets were still there. The jewelry box drawers were still open. The police had taken her body and left everything else just as the killer had—including the medallion crucifix that she kept in a bowl next to her bed.

He noticed it was turned over so that Jesus was face down.

Chuck was aghast. As he later told his buddy John Elwell: "My mother would never put it face down…and whoever did it…turned it over before he killed her so as to not do it in [the] eyes of Christ."

Did the police notice this? Did the crucifix point the finger at anyone?

Chuck *did* finally obtain the will from Ruth's attorney. But it took a while. Lowell Davies was not eager to meet with Chuck in the days following her murder. Not surprisingly, given all that Davies knew about Chuck, Davies was hostile. Chuck remembered: "He was unsympathetic to me."

In the will, he was pleased to see in writing: "I give my property as follows: A. If I am survived by my son CHARLES, the whole thereof to him."

He was soon appointed the executor of her estate. And it did not take long for Gunker to start spending her money. In May 1975, he began making a series of "loan" payments to himself from her estate: $6,000 on May 1; $200 on June 12; $300 on June 21; $500 on July 1; $350 on August 1 and then $37.10 on August 5; $400 on December 10; $4,194.35 on December 30 and then $1,857.72 on the following day, December 31; $1,000 on January 6, 1976; and then a paltry $31.65 ten days later, on January 16, 1976.

For the next twenty years, he listed his employment on his résumé as manager of his own investment portfolio. Like Hank, he lived off an inheritance. He was not a millionaire, but Ruth's $200,000 in securities and her $20,000 life insurance payout, if invested well, would provide him some income—for a while. Though he had fathered a daughter and a son, he had met neither and provided no financial support to either one.

He sold all of Ruth's possessions and went on a shopping spree, buying expensive tailored leisure suits, dress shoes, a gold watch and a sheepskin jacket. This was the height of 1970s culture: disco was coming, cocaine was replacing marijuana as the drug of choice and the New Age movement was luring Americans to Eastern religions and the Far East. Chuck was attracted. A year after Ruth's death, in 1976, he took off on an extended trip to visit Chuck McDougal, a.k.a. the "Tiger Man." A fellow Coronado boy and avid body surfer, McDougal was a world-renowned tiger expert. He conducted his research at Tiger Tops in Chitwan National Park in Nepal. When he invited Chuck to join him in Nepal, Chuck jumped at the chance. After all, he now had the funds for adventures.

24

UNRESOLVED

I'm not scared, because I don't have anything to lose. They've got all the money and all the big lawyers and all the worries. I'm just being happy with a small mentality that says just live every day and have a good time with your kids and your life.
—*Alan Graham, in an interview with Gary James of ClassicBands.com*

Wearing a black beret over his long, gray locks, with a large blue scarf wrapped around his neck and sporting purple shoes, Alan Graham serenaded shoppers entering and exiting the Vons supermarket on Orange Avenue in Coronado. A gray-bearded friend in tow, he strummed the guitar and sang songs about Jim Morrison; his first love, "Anna" (as he called her); and his conflicts with her father, Admiral Morrison. Cars and clattering shopping carts dodged him. He crooned: "I roamed around this Coronado town. Mined for diamonds on her silver sands. But still she waits. Praise her love unbound."

He *was* roaming around, as he seemed to have no home of his own. He had been kicked out of the apartment he shared with his second wife, and they were now estranged. He squatted for a few months on the floor of an antiques store on the island, where he slept on a bedroll and posted YouTube videos of his encampment and the whiskey bar he claimed he was setting up in the shop.

He was continuing his practice of ingratiating himself with people and then taking from them. He took over the store, selling inventory on the sidewalk. He stole jewelry from the store.

Former Coronado police officer Sergeant Bob Paseman says this fit a pattern with Alan. He was a lifelong thief, he claimed, snatching wallets and purses from islanders. And he was probably mentally ill or at least unstable.

Chuck believed so: "After my mother's death, I found lots of things in her effects, papers and things, and one of them was some poems Alan Graham had written. And I could tell from the poems he was very disturbed."

The owner of the antiques store was beside herself. Alan refused to leave. She eventually got rid of him by changing the locks. Angry, he harassed her with threatening phone calls.

Then a generous and wealthy lady friend, a Coca-Cola heiress and descendant of the founder of the Nunnally Candy Company (a boxed chocolate company known as "the candy of the south"), rescued him. She let him stay in her Coronado rental property, a ranch-style rambler near the ocean. He decorated the interior with Jim Morrison photographs and posters, a variety of masks, a mummy outfitted with a baseball cap, a disco glitter ball and a sign announcing: "Bomb Squad Vehicle Parking."

Alan Graham serenading shoppers at Vons grocery store in Coronado, 2023. *Joe Ditler.*

He called himself the Reverend Alan Graham, doing podcast interviews in his beret, a big crucifix around his neck and a Sgt. Pepper's–style band conductor jacket. He was a religious man, he claimed, an altar boy as a child and a practicing Catholic. And he told everyone that he started the "Ministry of Rock" in 1987, where he counseled those of all faiths, including Muslims. He was there to pray for everyone, he said.

Asked about the cameo theft he committed more than fifty years earlier, he became enraged and responded with vituperative threats: "You are reckless and dangerous. I will write an exposé about you!"

He died six months later without writing one. Cared for by hospice, he lived out his final days in the rental property. He lay propped up in a hospital bed in an unadorned bedroom with a single light bulb. As he was recorded for a Facebook video, he smiled from his deathbed while waving a butane lighter to the beat of "Light My Fire," which blared loudly in the background. Surrounded by three of his children, his estranged second wife, several squatters he had invited to live with him and thirteen stray dogs, Alan died in May 2024.

A funeral Mass was said for him at Sacred Heart, the same church where Ruth Quinn, Laura Christian and Hank Leyendecker were memorialized. Several people gave eulogies, including the family of a young man Alan mentored. According to the Graham family, he rescued young people and dogs his whole life.

"My dad was super charming with older people and young people, but not with people his own age," his son Sefton Graham said. Alan rarely took responsibility for his criminal behavior, but Sefton was one of the few people who could get his father to "own up" to his actions.

Was he capable of murder?

"The guy I know could not do it." He just did not see his dad holding a grudge for three years and *then* committing murder. His former brother-in-law Andy Morrison agreed: "I don't think he had murder in him." And Alan also had an alibi.

Was he a grifter?

Sefton has a different term: "He was a hustler. In his movie, he is the good guy, the Robin Hood."

25

THE END

I am going to follow Uncle Hank's advice: "Let sleeping dogs lie."
—Handwritten journal notes by Chuck Quinn, 2008

In the last twenty-five years of his life, Chuck lived close to the ocean, south of San Francisco. No longer able to afford his apartment near the financial district with its soaring property values, Chuck moved in 1998 to Pacifica, a small town with six miles of sandy coast that offered surfing, hiking and fishing. With a population of thirty-seven thousand, it was not much larger than Coronado.

He rented a tiny ground-level apartment in a small housing complex subsidized by the Catholic church. Situated on a hill overlooking the ocean, the front of the building boasted a panoramic Pacific view. Chuck's apartment, however, was on the back side of the building, with a view of a dense forest of redwood trees. A tall concrete wall surrounding his patio fenced him in, keeping his abode shaded and secure. In this small, dark outside space, he was able to keep a few abalone shells filled with water and birdseed. In the twilight of his life, the birds continued to bring him a daily dose of joy, much as they had for his mother.

Inside his apartment, the air was stale. And after decades of hoarding all his letters, journals, records, documents and handwritten notes, his apartment was crammed full of boxes: boxes covering all the kitchen counters, boxes lining the living room walls and boxes piled in the corners of his bedroom.

Could he be considered neurodivergent? Might such a diagnosis explain his childlike fascination with birds and trains? Could it clarify his fastidiousness and his obsession and compulsion with note keeping and file stashing? It would have been rare for any teacher or coach of his generation or older to have identified this condition. But it might account for some of his behavior.

His home was also filled with religious icons: a painting of the Virgin Mary and Jesus, several crucifixes—including one lying in the center of his bed—and a photo of him shaking Pope John Paul II's hand.

Chuck surrounded himself with photos and memorabilia of his life: a childhood portrait of him and little Michael, his parents' wedding day, his Navy discharge papers, a framed poster of his deep powder ski run that appeared in *National Geographic*, his diplomas and a candid of him and his daughter at their first meeting—when she was in her twenties. He also had a son, whom he met twice. And he recalled, "I'm aware of one grandchild that I held in my arms."

As a nonagenarian, Chuck was still standing tall and erect, but he did use the assistance of a tall walking stick. He wore a big crucifix around his neck and kept his safety deposit box key on a chain hanging from his belt—protected and always within reach.

He was no longer physically able to volunteer with the Missionaries of Charity on 29th Street in San Francisco, where he spent many years cleaning toilets, doing light carpentry work and even serving as a driver for Mother Teresa during her visits to San Francisco in the late 1980s—her head barely clearing the dashboard of his Mustang. He missed that era of his life: "The happiest time in my life was on 29th Street because it was so beautiful to give away love."

Asked about his family, he was eager to talk. And talk. And talk. He was notorious for being long-winded and for calling friends in the middle of the night to relive old memories and share stories about his family, the Heide and Quinn history, his father's World War II service, his brother's death—and his mother's murder. Tired of being awakened by his late-night ramblings, many of the recipients of these calls told him to stop contacting them.

Who did he believe murdered Ruth? For a long time, he had wondered about Hank.

"My mother was his meal ticket. She took care of him from the time that he was born...and so it was a dependency relationship between my mother and my uncle, which is sad and dangerous, you know, in that it breeds resentment in the one who is dependent. Tremendous resentment." Chuck would intimately understand that resentment.

Chuck Quinn on the patio of his apartment in Pacifica, California, 2022. *Author's collection.*

Tucked in his files was a newspaper article, clipped and saved since 1976. In it, a sociologist analyzed and described killers. Chuck carefully underlined a description of what the sociologist called "adversary situations." These cases, the article stated, involve "situations of long forbearance and hate, together with provocation or bold action by the victim that embarrasses the killer in front of others."

"My mom would whale on Hank," Chuck remembered. She would criticize him often and loudly, henpecking him, beating him down, to anyone and everyone. Chuck said she tried to make him look like a clown. And people around town felt sorry for Hank and how Ruth treated him. "He should have been man enough to fight back, but he didn't. I didn't have respect for her because of the way she treated her brother."

Chuck used to admonish Ruth: "I asked her, 'Why do you keep feeding him? Why do you let him come through the front door?'" If she hated him so, why did she keep her door open for him? And why did he keep coming back for more abuse?

While Hank allegedly never lost his temper with Ruth, Chuck did. "I used to have yelling matches with my mom." These fights were notorious, overheard by many neighbors.

He often wondered why the police were so dogged in their pursuit of him. Detective Dodson flew to San Francisco soon after the murder to search his San Francisco apartment. Dodson also flew to Carson City to interview Dr. Pat Flynn.

After that meeting, "I was the number one suspect." Why, Chuck reflected, were the police convinced of his guilt after their visit to Carson City? What did Pat say that made Chuck their target?

No matter. "I got it together and got off the hook." What did he mean? Was he able to prove where he was all day on Sunday, March 16, 1975? Or did the police just believe it was too implausible for him to have driven or flown to and from San Diego in one day?

Apparently his alibi stuck, because law enforcement turned their attention to Hank.

Ruth and Hank's relationship was just as fraught with venom as that between Ruth and Chuck. Everyone in town had heard the fights at one point or another. John Elwell remembered them vividly: "It was a madhouse at Ruth's where they met regularly for dinner. The dinners erupted, always, in screaming, violent, yelling arguments."

"That was the tragedy," Chuck said. "The tragedy was that my mother, she kept the door open for him and she would complain not just to me but to everybody in Coronado, belittling her brother, and I felt so sorry for him and that's why I thought that he might have erupted—and that dependency relationship."

At least she *had* a brother, he sometimes thought. Why did she take that relationship for granted?

But no one ever heard Hank raise his voice or lose his temper, except for Chuck: "Only one time at dinner one night, the three of us, did he lose his cool and he turned and said something like, 'Stop this.'"

At one point, Chuck wondered aloud: Could that dependency and resentment have fueled enough hatred to kill? Or could Hank have hired someone to kill Ruth? No, he resolved, Ruth was Hank's lifeline. "When things got bad, she was the one that took care of him. Like the time of my brother's death in 1939. What a dilemma: the horns of a dilemma....You can't win and you're going to get it one way or another."

By the end of his life Chuck had changed his mind. He agreed with Hank: the killer was Alan Graham. In a file Chuck saved until he died, he kept detailed records of every phone call and meeting he had in the weeks after his mother's death. There, he penciled in everything he learned about Alan: how he had met Ruth, who his brother-in-law was, who his father-in-law was and that he was a con man—even back in England.

With all that history and the fact that Alan orchestrated that robbery, Chuck believed, "It was a simple case."

Chuck Quinn also died in 2024, one month after Alan Graham. He fell and broke his hip and could no longer live independently. With the assistance of a kindly Heide cousin, he was admitted into a nursing home near the San Francisco Airport. Sharing a room with several other residents, he rested in a bed next to a sliding glass door, where he could look out to the parking lot and, in the distance, see the planes take off.

He could also see the birds. He would crack open the door and look at them longingly and listen to their tweets and chirps. As always, they soothed him. "I love birds because they can fly."

In the last few months of his life, he got depressed and angry about his mother's murder: "She was executed!" As his friend Esky Kurtz said of Chuck, "The bitterness was always there."

The lack of closure continued to nag at him, and he wondered aloud about his mother's culprit: "Why the hell haven't they caught the person? What did they do it for?"

He died of pneumonia at age ninety-one—almost eighty years after his father died of the same illness—without ever getting an answer.

Epilogue

THE DIRT

I'm a woman who can keep a secret.
—*Ruth Quinn, in a 1972 court deposition for the trial of the cameo theft*

W alking down the driveway toward 511 Pomona Avenue on a moonlit night, I noticed that the home's porch light was on—unlike the night of Ruth's murder fifty years ago. There are now more streetlights and a lot more cameras in the neighborhood, so the block is probably more illuminated and monitored than it was in 1975.

It was very still. The wind dies down at night in Coronado and the insects are silent. You cannot hear the ocean from Pomona Avenue, but you can occasionally make out the trains at the depot in downtown San Diego, across the bay. But not tonight.

Crowded by much larger homes (torn down and rebuilt over time), the cottage where Ruth lived and died looks like a 1930s relic.

And it is. It remains unchanged. The owners still call it "Ruth Quinn's house." The screen door is still rusty, and the siding needs a fresh coat of paint. The carport is 1960s vintage. The plum and crab apple trees in the yard are more mature, almost overgrown. And the patio fence is listing.

Islanders still talk about the murder of Ruth Quinn, especially those who were living here in 1975. Over coffee or cocktails, the old-timers posit their theories. Everyone has one: Chuck killed her for the money. Alan killed her out of revenge. Hank killed her, in a fit of rage and hatred, after years of pent-up anger and resentment. Locals are about evenly divided over the culpability of the three main suspects—all of whom are dead.

Some believe a hit man was hired to do the job. Could it have been a killer contracted by one of the above? Or could it have been one of the neighbors or their children, several of whom still live in the neighborhood?

Could the real killer still be alive and living on the island?

Law enforcement is convinced Hank is the culprit. It was a crime of passion, they argue, committed by someone who had reached his boiling point with the victim.

But those who knew Hank shake their heads in disbelief. They are not convinced that a man like Hank—alternatively described as "ineffectual," a "mama's boy," a "man's man," a "confirmed bachelor" and even "a queen, light in his loafers"—was capable of such a violent act. They never saw him lose his temper.

Hank remains an enigma. With few first-person accounts available, it is difficult to ascertain his state of mind. When Hank died in 1984, Laura Christian's children Valerie Quate and Kemp Christian cleaned out his apartment. Other than his belt buckle and Lucinda, he did not own much of value. They never found "the book," the journal where he claimed he kept a record of his life.

And where is the gun?

Ruth's home is just a block away from the on-ramp to the Coronado Bridge: a quick escape. And throwing a gun out the window at nighttime as you ascend the big arch and speed over the San Diego Harbor would be relatively easy. In 1975, the outbound nighttime traffic was light.

A block away from Ruth's home is the Coronado golf course that lines Glorietta Bay on the south side of the Bridge. It would have been relatively simple to walk to its edge and toss in a gun. The course is not well lit. Who knows how many secrets are buried in the muck at the bottom of the island's harbor?

Or it could be hidden away in a bank safety deposit box—if the owner of that box is still paying the rent. Or it could be hidden away in someone's home. Could the gun still be on the island?

In 2006, a San Diego homicide detective named Victor Caloca reopened this very cold case for a few months and reexamined the evidence before closing it again. In 2023, two cold case detectives in San Diego reopened the case once more. They cited evidence that could, with more advances in technology, be tested for DNA. The large DNA databases housed at ancestry.com and 23andme.com have made it possible to identify killers or their close relatives.

But, as the sergeant reminded me, "We would still have to place the suspect at the scene of the crime."

The scene of the crime: a little cottage and patio that Ruth rented for $175 a month. Today, it is hard to find a freestanding home with outdoor space in Coronado for less than $10,000 a month. And the dirt underneath any one of these homes is worth millions of dollars.

Did Ruth hear her killer approach when he (or she) interrupted her quiet repose that day? She was probably lying on her left side, curled in a relaxed fetal position when the first shot through the pillow entered the meaty part of her right collarbone—exiting the left side of her neck. This might account for the smeared blood that was found on the left side of her face and on her left hand.

But this first shot did not kill her. As she most likely roiled in agony, did she open her eyes and see her killer before he smothered her head again with the pillow and fired that second and fatal shot behind her right ear?

Ruth was hoping to live a few more years, in peace, on her island paradise, passing away her final days on her little piece of Coronado dirt. Someone stole that from her. And got away with it.

A TIMELINE OF THE MURDER

Sunday, March 16, 1975

Times are all approximate, based on police interviews with the suspects or based on witness accounts.

Early morning   Chuck Quinn leaves Dr. Pat Flynn's family home in Carson City, Nevada, to go hiking or skiing with some friends.

11:00 a.m.   Ruth Quinn attends Mass at Sacred Heart Catholic Church, followed by a church breakfast.

1:15–2:15 p.m.   Hank Leyendecker shares a meal with his girlfriend Laura Christian at her home at 1015 Encino Row.

3:15 p.m.   A fellow parishioner arrives at Ruth's home to deliver flowers and stays approximately thirty minutes.

3:30 p.m.   Hank Leyendecker leaves Laura's house, saying he's heading to the Millers at 732 B Avenue, the home where he rents a room.

3:30/4:00 p.m.   Ruth's landlord Cynthia "Cinnie" Heyer speaks to Ruth at her home about a leaky roof.

4:00 p.m.   Joe Ditler enters the driveway from Glorietta Boulevard looking for Ezra Parker. Told Ezra is at Ruth's house, Joe knocks on Ruth's door. There is no answer, but he hears the television.

4:00/4:30 p.m.   A witness, Betty Burns, sees Ruth at the library.

4:15 p.m.   Charlie and Bill White, eleven and twelve, of 500 Pomona Avenue, are skateboarding and observe Hank Leyendecker walking north on Pomona Avenue and entering Ruth's home. They continue skateboarding until approximately 8:00 p.m. They never see him leave.

4:30 p.m.   Ruth attends evening Mass.

Evening   Alan Graham and Anne Morrison Graham attend a dinner party at Mrs. Edinger's house on C Avenue with Kitty and Owen Chandler.

6:00 p.m.   A witness, Mrs. Burda, observes Ruth at church again, alone, praying.

6:30/6:40 p.m.   Laura Christian reports that Hank Leyendecker returns to her home.

6:45–7:00 p.m.   A neighbor at 522 Glorietta Boulevard, Louis Niles, reports that he hears gunshots.

6:57 p.m.   Sunset and taps.

7:45–9:15 p.m.   Katheryn Lloyd says she calls Ruth four times to thank her for attending a retirement party on March 14. Each time, the phone is busy.

10:15/10:20 p.m.   Hank says he arrives at Ruth's house and finds Ruth's body. He calls family doctor Dr. Charles Eaton and Laura Christian and Monsignor John Purcell and waits outside the house. Dr. Eaton and his wife arrive, and on viewing Ruth's body, Dr. Eaton calls the Coronado

Police Department. Laura Christian and Monsignor Purcell arrive.

10:32 p.m.   Officer Don Erbe and Sergeant Dick Solomon arrive at the scene. They call Chief Art LeBlanc, who also arrives. Detective Paul Dodson arrives and waits with Ruth's body until the coroner arrives.

Late Sunday night or early Monday morning   The Coronado Police Department calls Dr. Pat Flynn's family home in Carson City looking for Chuck. They tell Pat Flynn that Ruth has been murdered.

Sometime Sunday night or early Monday morning   Chuck returns to the Flynn family home.

Monday, March 17, 1975

11:30 a.m.   Dr. Pat Flynn tells Chuck that Ruth has been murdered.

12:06 p.m.   The Coronado Police Department receives a phone call from Chuck Quinn, saying he heard about the murder "from a friend."

BIBLIOGRAPHY

This book is a work of nonfiction, based on many primary and secondary sources, including books, magazines, web sites, newspaper archives and emails to and from various primary sources. In some instances, primary sources preferred to be interviewed on background or anonymously.

Books

Atlantic City (NJ) Gazette-Review. "Who's Who in the Hotel Supply World." October 13, 1922. newspapers.com.

Butler, Pamela. *Angels Dance and Angels Die*. New York: Schirmer Trade Books, 1998.

Carlin, Katherine Eitzen, and Ray Brandes. *Coronado: The Enchanted Island*. Coronado, CA: Coronado Historical Association, 1998.

Davis, Stephen. *Jim Morrison: Life, Death, Legend*. New York: Gotham Books, 2005.

Elwell, John C., Jane Schmauss and the California Surf Museum. *Surfing in San Diego*. Charleston, SC: Arcadia Publishing, 2007.

Ewing, Steve. *Reaper Leader: The Life of Jimmy Flatley*. Annapolis, MD: U.S. Naval Institute Press, 2002.

———. *Thach Weave: The Life of Jimmie Thach*. Annapolis, MD: U.S. Naval Institute Press, 2004.

Ewing, Steve, and John B. Lundstrom. *Fateful Rendezvous: The Life of Butch O'Hare.* Annapolis, MD: U.S. Naval Institute Press, 1997.

Graham, Alan. *I Remember Jim Morrison Too.* Self-published memoir, 2022.

Hopkins, Jerry, and Danny Sugarman. *No One Here Gets Out Alive.* New York: Grand Central Publishing, 1980.

Hynes, Terry. *A Brief Biography of Muriel Claire Heide.* Self-published, 2022.

Nichols, Katherine. *Deep Water.* New York: Simon True, 2017.

Pye, Anne Briscoe, and Nancy Shea. *The Navy Wife.* New York and London: Harper & Brothers Publishers, 1942.

Ringley, Tom. *Wranglin' Notes: A Chronicle of Eatons' Ranch 1879–2010.* Greybull, WY: Pronghorn Press, 2010.

Journals, Magazines, Newspapers

Bearman, Joshuah. "Coronado High: A Legendary Drug-Smuggling Ring in a Sleepy California Town." *GQ,* September 8, 2013, https://www.gq.com.

Blair, Cynthia. "It Happened in New York." *Newsday* (New York, NY), January 28, 2005. newspapers.com.

Brannin, Jeannette. "Rare, Sacred Art Objects Displayed: USD Aide Assembles Salon of Treasure." *San Diego Union,* November 28, 1970.

Buckley, Marcie. "Police Chief—The Cerebral Cop." *Coronado Journal,* January 18, 1979.

Coronado Journal. "Paul Dodson Takes the Helm at Coronado Yacht Club." December 12, 2007.

———. "Polio Can Strike Your Neighbor." January 19, 1956.

Cromie, William J. "Killers—'Situation' Is the Culprit." *San Francisco Chronicle,* February 15, 1976.

Cross, Greta, "Decades After He 'Terrorized' Springfield in Support of Larry Flynt, Captain Pink Releases Books." *Springfield (Missouri) News Leader,* February 6, 2022.

Desjardins, Doug. "Surfing Craze Captured City in '60s." *Coronado Journal,* June 8, 1989.

Goffard, Christopher. "Joan Irvine Smith, Daughter of O.C. Land Baron Family Who Helped Establish UC Irvine, Dies at 86." *Los Angeles Times,* December 20, 2019. https://www.latimes.com.

"Heide—71 Years of Success." *Dextrose Digest* 3, no. 3 (1940): 3–13.

Heide, Sister Muriel, RSCJ. "A History of the Henry Heide family." In "A Brief Biography of Muriel Claire Heide," compiled by Terry Hynes, unpublished, 2022.

Los Angeles Times. "Rites Set for Doctor Eaton of Coronado." January 25, 1990. https://www.latimes.com.

New York Herald Tribune. "Michael Quinn Dies, 32 Years on Police Force, 'Strong Arm Mike,' 71, in Charge of W. 47th St. Detectives for a Time, Quit in '24, Ran Café, 6 Ft. 2 In. and 240 Pounds, He Served in 'Tough' Areas." 1937.

New York Telegram. "Quinn-Leyendecker." Wedding announcement. October 30, 1930.

New York Times. "Henry Heide Dead; Head of Candy Firm." December 14, 1931.

———. "Michael J. Quinn, Retired Detective, Cited for Meritorious Service Three Times in 32 Years—Dies at 71." October 6, 1937.

Patterson, Christine. "Sweet Success for 125 Years." *Central New Jersey Home News,* March 6, 1994.

Pokin, Steve. "Pokin Around: When Captain Pink and the Larry Flynt Circus Came to Springfield." *Springfield News-Leader,* February 14, 2021. https://www.news-leader.com.

Revis, Kathleen. "Skiing in the United States." *National Geographic Magazine,* February 1959.

San Diego Evening Tribune. "Child Killed by Truck in Coronado." July 27, 1939.

San Diego Union. "Cameo Theft Figure Given Unusual Term." *San Diego Union,* June 23, 1972.

———. "Coronado Man Convicted In Cameo Theft." May 19, 1972.

———. "3 Arrested in $50,000 Cameo Theft." January 12, 1972.

Times-Union (Brooklyn, NY). "Henry Heide's Estate Valued at $419,586 Net." February 14, 1934.

Wilkens, John. "Remembering San Diego's Shoe Bandit." *San Diego Union-Tribune,* September 17, 2016. https://www.sandiegouniontribune.com.

Wolfert, Ira. "The Silent, Invisible War Under the Sea." *Readers Digest,* November 1945.

Other Documents

Personal files of Chuck Quinn Jr. to include letters to and from Chuck Quinn, handwritten notes and diary entries, hotel and rental car and taxicab receipts, airline tickets, hospital records, telegrams, church and opera and funeral programs, obituaries, Alcoholics Anonymous membership and meeting records, newspaper and magazine articles, military service records and VA benefits documents, résumés, job applications, photographs, court documents, family and genealogy research records, bank and insurance and financial and credit card statements and safety deposit box records.

Coroner's Report #72009, Office of the Coroner, County of San Diego, April 23, 1975.

Graham, A.R. *Poet Rain.* Coronado, CA: Windward Press, 1973.

Grand Jury testimony given by Ruth Quinn to Steven B. Davis, Deputy District Attorney, County of San Diego, 1972.

Letter from Alan R. Graham to Ruth Quinn, June 13, 1972.

Websites

CandyBlog. "Jujyfruits & Jujubes." http://www.candyblog.net/blog/item/jujyfruits_jujubes.

Consumer Grouch. "A NYC Candy Maker Extraordinaire." December 24, 2022. https://www.consumergrouch.com/?p=9623.

Coronado Historical Association. coronadohistory.org.

Facebook profiles of Alan Graham and Kimberly Dill Graham.

James, Gary. Interview with Alan Graham. Classic Bands. https://www.classicbands.com/AlanGrahamInterview.html.

Kermit & Friends Zone. "Jim Morrison Murdered?! His Brother-in-Law Says So!" YouTube, June 13, 2022. https://www.youtube.com/watch?v=b9KAMb_V0G4.

Nicholson, Helge. "Interview with Jim Morrison's Father and Sister." YouTube, August 9, 2010. https://www.youtube.com.

Strange Planet. "The Real Jim Morrison with Alan Graham." YouTube, November 3, 2017. https://www.youtube.com.

Interviews and Emails

Most of these interviews were conducted by the author. Some were conducted by Joe Ditler. Some were conducted by both. Emails were transmitted between sources and author and/or Joe Ditler.

Barbara Beardsley
Michael Callahan
Victor Caloca
Steve Collins
Joe Ditler
Paul Dodson
John Elwell
Rear Admiral Jim Flatley
Monica Flynn
Pat Flynn
Vince Flynn
Alan Graham
Sefton Graham
Richard Hartwell
Heide and Quinn family cousins
Bob Hutton
Deena Jones-Webber
Susan Keith

Esky Kurtz
Art LeBlanc
Clara Mason
Hal Matthews
Pike Meade
Michael Moret
Maureen Moriarty
Andy Morrison
John Morton
Caroline Murray
Bob Paseman
Shannon Player
Valerie Quate
Chuck Quinn
Doug St. Denis
Dick Tarbuck
Former neighbor of Ruth Quinn
Owner of Coronado antiques store

ABOUT THE AUTHOR

T aylor Baldwin Kiland, a former naval officer, is the third generation in her family to serve in the Navy and live in Coronado, California.

She is the author, coauthor or ghostwriter of more than twenty books, mostly in the military nonfiction genre and, specifically, about Vietnam prisoners-of-war and their families. She has occasionally written some children's books, including one picture book about Coronado: *Oz, Dog of the Del*.

Taylor lives in Old Town Alexandria, Virginia, with her husband and daughter, but she visits the island about once a month to check on her dad.

Murder of the Jujube Candy Heiress: A Coronado Cold Case is her first cold case murder mystery. Learn more about her at TaylorKiland.com.

Author in her Coronado Soccer League uniform, 1977. *Author's collection.*